LOVE BULLSH!T

Anaimir Publishing
www.lovebullshit.com

Copyright © 2024 Ana Bakotic

All rights reserved. No part of this book may be reproduced, distributed, or transmitted in any form or by any means, including photocopying, recording, or other electronic or mechanical methods, without the prior written permission of the publisher, except in the case of brief quotations embodied in critical reviews and certain other non-commercial uses permitted by copyright law. For permission requests, write to info@lovebullshit.com.

Publisher: Anaimir Publishing
England, UK

ISBN: 978-1-0685812-0-5

This book is a work of nonfiction. The events and discussions are drawn from personal experiences, insights, and research. Any resemblance to actual persons, living or dead, or actual events is purely coincidental.

Cover Design: Ana Bakotic

First Edition: December 2024

For more information, visit **www.lovebullshit.com**.

Are you ready?

Hi!

I am a book about love, but not about all the bullshit that everyone is used to calling 'love'. I am a book about real, unconditional love.

So many lives have been taken in the name of love, so much pain has been given in the name of love. I believe it's time to stop with that bullshit and create a completely new world full of real love.

Many of you think you know what love is. You might even call yourselves 'love experts'. I am inviting you to have a go at this, for some, completely new perspective of love, before you try to love, or before you try to love again.

Please don't be confused by my unusual form. I don't have a table of contents or chapters, on purpose. Also, I was written in the form of a dialogue, a dialogue between self and a higher self.

Read me, apply me, read me again. Every time you read me, I will become even more clear. Every time you apply me...well, you'll see.

My goal is a world in which every single person is full of tolerance and understanding, a world in which every single person is creative, productive, and contributes to its development, a world full of real love, peace, joy and abundance, a world that blooms.

Because we are all one, I know that this kind of world is also your goal. So let's do it! It's time.
Are you with me?

Of course! How do we recognise what real love is?

Many people would agree that love can be recognised by acts and not words, but it's not that easy. There are many acts of 'love' that are not love and many acts that appear not to be love, which are indeed love.

Hmmm?

So it is not about *what* you do, but from which place you are doing it. Let me explain this one. When I say a 'place', I don't think about a physical location, I think about your inner state. Before you say or do something, ask yourself if you are doing this from a state of inner peace, joy and abundance, or if it's something else.

Something else?

Well, many people would say: 'I worry about them because I love them, I am angry because I love them, I am dying because I love them, I am protecting them because I love them, I am helping them because I love them...' My dear friend, worry, anger and dying don't have anything to do with love, and most of the time, neither do protecting and helping.

Whaaat?

I know, I know. I will explain myself. Love is not what we say, do, or even feel. Love is a state of being. Our natural state of being. In other words, love is who we really are. I believe that only when we connect with our inner peace, joy and/or abundance, we are our real selves. I would say that we *are* love, and whenever we act from this inner peace, joy and abundance, we are being ourselves.

So why are we not ourselves always?

During the first seven years of our lives, we experience many things that make us forget who we really are. Just being small in a world of big, busy and tired people, makes us believe that we are vulnerable, weak, unimportant, not valuable, not worthy, not deserving, not loved, not enough, etc. That gets stuck in our subconscious mind, so when we grow up, even though none of that is true, we still believe we are all those things.

So what can we do about it?

We need to remember who we really are, but not just on the conscious level, we also need to remind our subconsciousness who we really are.

You mean love?

Exactly! Also, we need to remember how it is to *be* love. What it is like.

Do you mean peaceful, joyful and abundant?

Yes, but also protected, loved, safe, strong, powerful, valuable, worthy, enough, complete...

How are we going to feel protected, loved, safe, etc. if we are not?

Who said we are not? We are!

Wait a minute. If we are protected, loved, safe, and all that, why then, do we see all these horrible things going on in the world?

You see what you believe.

So you want me to ignore all the terrible things going on in the world, like they are just in my imagination?

I want you to stop feeding them or, better yet, I want you to stop feeding your subconscious false beliefs about yourself with them.

What does any kind of belief about myself have to do with wars, murders, rapes, thefts, etc.?

Let's imagine all that is real. It's not but, on some level it is, just not on the important one.

What do you mean 'it's not real'?

All those horrible things are lies that we tell ourselves about our world to justify how we feel inside.

What are you talking about?!

I am saying that you don't feel what you see. You see what you feel.

So, I am like a crazy person creating my own reality?

No, you are like a normal person creating your own reality. We all do it. We are all creating our reality, non-stop, regardless of whether we are aware of that or not.

If everything around us is an illusion, why does it feel so real?

How does a dream feel when you sleep? Just as real, until you wake up. Likewise, this illusion feels real, until you wake up.

So how will I awaken? Is it a physical death that is waking me up?

Oh no, your awakening is already in the process. Just by talking about it, asking and expressing an interest is proof that you are already waking up.
Even when you are awakening from a physical dream, at one point, you accept that it was a dream.

Thus, this awakening is largely based on accepting the existence of the dream, and then comes an effort to open your eyes to the truth. The one that I mentioned at the beginning about your essence being peace, joy and abundance, being love.

The death of the body has nothing to do with awakening. Many leave this body still dreaming.

But let's now return to the assumption that this reality is, indeed, real. What now with those horrors of this world? What can you do? Can you, the individual, end it?

I don't see that I can. Maybe I can contribute a little bit to its end.

So in what way do you think you can contribute the best?

Well... with donations, protests, volunteering...

All that is nice, except most people do those things to wash away their 'sins' and sense of guilt, and not to really help.

Why do you say 'sins' and not sins?

Because sins don't exist. There is no such thing as afterlife punishment. No one punishes you, or can ever punish you, except you yourself by depriving yourself of peace, joy and abundance. What you call sins are actions that have punishment as a consequence, but I believe 'punishment' comes first, and 'sin' is just a reaction from a miserable state of being.

So protesting, donating and volunteering can make you feel superficially better, but no, they can't end the horrors in this world.

So what can then? What can I do as an individual?

Work on eliminating all those horrors in you.

Wait, there is no war and injustice in me.

(a sceptic side-eye look)

Maybe a little bit of injustice, but not war, and definitely not like there is in the world.

How much smaller are you than the planet? Compared with your size, there are even more wars in you than on the entire planet. Everyone fights their own wars, only they are not aware of it. War with neighbours, war with family, with government, war with oneself, the list goes on. If everyone would make an effort to end that internal war and learn unconditional love, the world would be in peace and prosperity.

So, I should be the first to change, not the other side. So, I am always the guilty one?

I didn't say that. That's what your childhood trauma hears what I said, in a way that it can be fed. Can you see now how it works? I didn't mention guilt at all, but your belief in your own sinfulness makes you perceive that's what I said.

Oh, I get it now. We see what we believe, and we believe what we experienced in our first seven years of life. It is all subconscious, that's why we are not even aware of it. So, you're telling me that love is more like our inner state, our essence, that we experience peace, joy and abundance, expressed through our words and actions, and that the reason why we are not aware of this essence of ours, all the time, is because of those false beliefs about ourselves created in our first seven years.

Exactly! Some of those beliefs can even be adopted while we are in our mother's womb or they can be inherited from our ancestors.

Interesting! So what's the easiest way to check if we truly love someone? Is it when someone treats us well and makes us feel happy, that 'happiness in action' is love?

Not at all. The peace, joy and abundance that I am talking about don't come from outside of you and don't depend on anything from outside either. That's an illusion. The Illusion is believing that you are beautiful because someone told you that, or that you are amazing because someone told you that. You are beautiful because you are, and you are amazing because you are!

Beautiful and amazing?

Just because you are.

Just...because...you are. Can you feel the peace in that? Being is enough. You don't need to do or achieve anything to prove yourself, because you are. That awareness of unconditional self-worth brings peace, joy and abundance and not what someone is telling you. Whatever someone is saying about you, good or bad, doesn't have any importance and can't change in any way what you really are. Whenever you rest your value on what people are saying about you, you are lying to yourself. It doesn't matter how happy that makes you feel, it also makes you feel vulnerable, because, if that person changes their opinion, you are going to be devastated. So, that kind of happiness is not love, the same as it is not the one that arises from any kind of achievement. The moment you permit yourself to feel proud and happy because you achieved something, you automatically condemn yourself for every failure you have had. Achievement-based happiness is the illusion that you are worthy only if you achieve something, and that is not true. You are unconditionally worthy, beautiful, amazing, great, important, and so much more, just because you are.

Wow! That sounds nice! Liberating!

Peaceful, joyful and abundant?

Yeah!!!

That's the answer to your previous question about the easiest way to check if we truly love someone. Every time you are in peace, joy or abundance, you love, because from that state of being, whatever you do, say or think, will be love. So in order to truly love, just allow yourself to experience peace, joy and abundance.

Ha, 'allow yourself'. Easy to say, but how? I mostly feel worried and miserable, stressed and exhausted. Far away from peace, joy and abundance.

I know. That's because you forget who you are. Try this! Repeat after me, and after saying it, take a few seconds to try to feel it as much as possible.

OK

I am

I am

Peaceful

Peaceful

I am

I am

Joyful

Joyful

I am

I am

Abundant

Abundant

Because

Because

I am

I am

Love

Love

I am peaceful

I am peaceful

I am joyful

I am joyful

I am abundant

I am abundant

Because I am love.

Because I am love.

I am peaceful, I am joyful, I am abundant, because I am love.

I am peaceful, I am joyful, I am abundant, because I am love.

I am peaceful, I am joyful, I am abundant, because I am love.

I am peaceful, I am joyful, I am abundant, because I am love.

I am peaceful, I am joyful, I am abundant, because I am love.

I am peaceful, I am joyful, I am abundant, because I am love.

So? How do you feel?

Absolutely peaceful, joyful and abundant.

You see. It always works if you open yourself properly to it and try to feel it. Was it challenging to feel it in the beginning?

A lot. When we started, my focus was terrible. I was able to think of everything except what we were saying. But I kept trying, I focused harder and the focus led me to feel it better. It really feels like peace, joy and abundance were always in me.

Because they were, they are and they will always be. With a focus on your essence, on what you really are, you are breaking those layers that prevent you from seeing and experiencing the real you.

What if I forget, again, who I am?

Remind yourself again and again, until you completely break all the layers of who you are not.

So how often?

No one knows. Keep yourself aware of your inner state. Be honest and brave to admit that you forgot again, and then repeat what we just did. It doesn't matter if you need to repeat it every day, every hour or every half an hour. Just do it!

Sounds simple.

It is, but your layers will fight. Your false self will try to convince you otherwise. For example, every time you decide to observe your feelings, when you find something that is not love, your old you will judge you and make you feel guilty, which will prevent you from facing this layer and dealing with it. The guilt will be so strong that you will convince yourself that you feel good, even if you don't, only because the pain of the guilt will be stronger than anything else. But whatever you feel, no matter how uncomfortable and painful it is, it is not your fault. You just forgot who you are, but it is not your fault and there is no need to judge yourself.

So who's fault is it?

No one's. Whoever was part of the first seven years of your life, they also weren't aware of who they really are, as they also had in the first seven years of their lives someone who hadn't known who they really are, and so on. Do you get it? It is no one's fault. We are all innocent. All of us.

I think I get it. I received those false beliefs about myself from my family and they from their family and they from their family, but when you say 'all of us', do you mean every single person in this world?

Yes!

Wait a minute! That sounds nice, but it is a little bit difficult to accept that everyone is innocent, including those who kill.

I know, but when you truly understand that no one is hurting anyone on purpose, then you will understand that everyone is innocent.

What are you talking about? That can't be true! I am sure many people are evil. They are just looking for someone to hurt.

That is exactly what your trauma wants you to see! Your perception of evil people exists only to justify the victimism in you. As soon as you heal the victimism trauma, you will be able to see that everyone is innocent. Try it for a second. Just ignore your victimism and imagine that no one is evil. Open yourself to that idea. To the idea that no one is looking for someone to hurt. They are only looking for a way to release their emotional pain.

Hmm...

Listen, we all have different false self-beliefs. Someone's false beliefs are stronger and bigger than someone else's. All those false beliefs create pain and discomfort. Have you ever yelled at someone?

Unfortunately, yes.

Before you started to yell, did you think 'I am going to hurt you now and humiliate you by yelling at you' or was it just some kind of discomfort or even emotional pain that arose from the inside and that you wanted to release?

The pain. Definitely the pain.

Can you now suppose how that pain can be much, much, much bigger in some people?

I believe so, yes.

Can you now understand how no one is ever doing anything to hurt anyone? They just do whatever horrible things they do, to release their own pain.

So, does that, whatever they do, actually help them to release their pain?

Does yelling release yours?

I don't think so. On some level, it makes it go away, but, on another, it makes it worse.

Exactly! It is the same as taking alcohol or drugs. The illusion of the release. It makes it worse in the long run, because it hides the problem, instead of healing it. The only way to heal that pain is by becoming aware of it, accepting it and letting it go with the understanding that it is only part of an illusion and not the real you. Drugs, alcohol, yelling, hurting, killing... These things are taking you deeper into the illusion. It is an illusion inside the illusion. To wake up, you need to have the courage to face whatever you feel, instead of trying to escape from that.

Hmmm, makes sense. Also, it makes sense that we are all innocent and that no one hurts anyone on purpose, now that you explained it that way, but have you ever heard this: 'The greatest trick the devil ever played was convincing the world that he doesn't exist'?

Of course I have! That's one of the greatest jokes I've ever heard. The real quote should go like this: 'The greatest trick the devil ever played was convincing the world that he *does* exist.' Don't you get it? We invented the devil to be able to blame someone for how we feel, instead of taking responsibility for our emotions and dealing with them. It is always easier to blame someone. Let me ask you something. Have you ever had a cramp in your calves?

Yes. It's horrible. So painful and long-lasting.

Do you know what you need to do to release the pain in a few seconds?

Noooo. Tell me!

The cramp is an involuntary contraction. To release the pain, you need to make the contraction go away, which is actually to stretch the muscle, in this case, the calves. So, you can grab your toes and pull them towards your knee, or if you can't reach your toes, stand up by having the painful leg behind and then lean forward with your whole body to bring your back knee closer to your toes.

Uh, that will make it even more painful. I've already tried something similar.

How long did you do it?

Like a millisecond. It is so much more painful than the cramp itself.

You see, if you are able to face that bigger pain, for just a few seconds, the pain starts to release, and if you keep stretching it for a little bit longer, it goes away.

Really? Wow! I didn't know that.

Don't worry. Many people don't. I explained all this to actually help you understand how taking responsibility for our emotions and dealing with them feels the same. It is painful, very painful, but it takes no time, only courage. All this 'blaming others' thing, or inventing the devil to be able to blame someone, is not helping at all.

OK. I get it! We shouldn't blame anyone for how we feel. Whatever we feel, it's ours and we need to deal with it, but it's still very difficult not to judge people for what they do. You know when you see on the news, how people kill each other or torture each other... I understand that my sadness, from that moment, is not their fault. My sadness is mine, I really get that part. Whatever I see is just helping me realise that I have sadness inside, from my past, but I can't ignore the fact that whatever I see is actually happening somewhere, so judging those who kill and attack is natural. Isn't it?

No, it's not. Judging is anything but natural. It doesn't matter if you judge your neighbours, mother-in-law, daughter-in-law or a nation. Every time we judge someone or something, it is because our focus is not on love and abundance, it is on scarcity. You perceive the lack of something. You are feeding your false beliefs again.

But this is not about me.

Everything is about you. The way you see the world around you is the way you feel inside you. That doesn't mean if you perceive your neighbour as rude, that you are rude as well. That means that if you perceive your neighbour as rude, your false belief about yourself might be that you are sensitive and vulnerable.

OK, OK, but what if my neighbour is really rude?

Maybe they are, but if you didn't have that false belief about your vulnerable and sensitive self, you wouldn't have even noticed them being rude. And especially, you wouldn't have noticed it so much, that it would make you judge them.

OK. I get that. But what about war? How can that be only a perception?

Even more so, given how you saw that on the news. I really recommend you not to watch any kind of news. It will not help you at all to remember who you are. Everything you see on the news is even less real than what you can see in person, because what you see is information filtered through those who participated in creating that news and those are mostly a bunch of people who live in the same state of scarcity as many others in this world. Even those who live the war in person, don't know what's going on. So how can the news be the source of truth?

I know, but if I stop watching or reading the news, I will become isolated and ignorant, and will not know what's going on in the world.

So?

Well... for example, how can I help by ignoring the situation?

How are you helping now, by watching it?

I don't know. I am not, but I feel like I should do something. Ignoring it seems very selfish. At least I could sympathise with the victim.

Precisely! Most of the people watch the news and don't do anything. Do you think that sympathising helps? Do you think that the victim even knows or cares that you are sympathising? Sympathising is probably the most selfish thing you can do.

No way!

Sympathising with any victim, even with your poor friend who was just left by their partner, is nothing else but selfish feeding of your false beliefs. We are all addicts to all those chemical formulas flowing through our bodies when we feed our false beliefs. I like to call us 'Emotionaholics'. Every victim we see is an opportunity for another shot. That's why everyone likes the news so much. The more negative they are, the better, because the shot is bigger.

Let me tell you something. Every time you are sympathising with a victim, you are actually judging someone.

I don't understand.

If there is a victim, then there is a perpetrator. No victim can exist without a perpetrator. A perpetrator is always judged, disliked or even hated. Would you say that the feeling of those is joyful and peaceful? Can anyone judge, dislike or hate someone with joy and peace, or from the feeling of abundance?

Of course not.

Do you think that the perpetrator hurts the victim from joy, peace and abundance?

I don't think so.

So, who do we actually help by abandoning our joy, peace and abundance?

Probably no one.

Exactly! You can also say that we are actually helping the illusion. Which means we are producing more pain and suffering every time we judge.

I always thought that judging someone who deserves it makes justice, a balance in the universe and protects the victim.

Many people think that way, but I believe the truth is quite the opposite. Let's imagine there is a war between good and bad. I don't believe in such a thing, but it will help me to explain the judging thing. Most people believe that, when they judge, they are good, because they are taking a good side. Let's imagine that this war between good and bad is like a war between light and darkness. I suppose you see yourself as a light warrior?

Definitely!

Well, if we agree that light is like peace, joy and abundance. Pure love! And darkness, like unrest, pain and scarcity. Pure fear! Do you think with judging, we feed light or darkness?

Darkness.

Do you see how judging someone converts you into a warrior of darkness? Every time you judge, you are feeding darkness, you are helping darkness to win the war.

Right. Makes sense. So, what should I do to stop feeding the darkness, when I find myself in a situation where it is obvious who the bad guy is?

It is never obvious who the bad guy is, because the bad guy doesn't exist, only the lost one. So what you should do is forgive. Forgiveness will liberate you from the darkness, and you will automatically feed the light, by which I mean, bring more peace, joy and abundance into the world.

So, why did you say that you don't believe in the war between the good and bad, if it's clear that we feed all the time the good or the bad side?

Just as good and bad guys don't exist, also the good or bad sides don't exist. What we feed is the truth or the illusion. Everything you see as bad, dark, destructive or negative is only an illusion. A dream! I used the war comparison only to explain myself better, but there is no war between the good and bad, because there is no good and bad. There is only awakening.

So even when I am judging, I am not feeding the darkness?

Exactly! You are feeding the illusion. You are only making up, dreaming, hallucinating... Forgiveness will make you see the truth.

I get it, but forgiving someone who is clearly hurting someone is so difficult.

It is not, if you remember that no one is hurting anyone on purpose. They are doing it to release their pain. By judging them, you are converting yourself into them and helping them to have more pain and to keep hurting more people.

Wow! That makes complete sense. I am only afraid that if I forgive someone who hurt me, I will become a victim again.

Forgiveness is a deep understanding of others' innocence and not a permission for more pain. Forgiveness is a deep understanding that no one can actually hurt *you*, but rather just feed the illusion of your vulnerability. Forgiveness is a deep understanding that we are all one, and that each of us is an equally valuable part of oneness, regardless of how lost some of us are. Forgiveness is a straight path to peace, joy and abundance. It is a straight path to love. Real love. Unconditional love. Forgiveness is a path to your true self.

Wow! I love this. Especially that 'each of us is an equally valuable part of oneness'. I love how it sounds. It's still a bit difficult to accept it for each and every one of us, but I get it. I get it even though I am not there yet. I don't feel it yet.

Of course! That's understandable. You are awakening but still not awake. I think that your mental openness to it is absolutely amazing! Unfortunately, many people can't yet see it on any level. So be proud of yourself. The more you try to apply what you have just learned, the more you will start to feel it and live it as well.

I believe so. Can you please explain to me a little bit more about oneness? I don't remember you mentioning it before. Is it something that some call God?

I don't know. It depends on what some people believe God is. If we talk about God as some separate entity far away from us, who only judges and punishes, then no. Oneness is definitely not that. I use the oneness word only to express the entity that includes us all. It is really important to understand the amazing connection between all of us. Without understanding that connection, we can't understand love. Do you remember when you asked me how we know that we truly love someone?

Yes, and you told me that every time we are peace, joy or abundance, we love; and that whatever we do, say or think, from that state of being, is love.

Absolutely! Well done! But the answer to this question also lies in the understanding of oneness and us as its equally valuable parts.

Why?

Because love is absolute! You can't love someone and not love someone else. You are loving or not loving. You can't love someone more than someone else. It is against love's true nature. You are the love. So you are expressing love or you are denying your true self. Because you are the love, you are not choosing who to love or not. You are just expressing your love through words and actions from the state of peace, joy and abundance; and your expression of love is not measured by how you treat one person, but how you treat everyone you meet or think about, divided by the number of those.

So, you are saying that I should love everyone equally?

Yes. On the surface of our awareness, we perceive the duality of existence, in which there is a sense of self, and then there is everything and everyone else. Basically, we perceive ourselves as existing separately from everyone and everything else. From this state of superficial awareness, when we feel that someone appears to be in a similar state of being to ours, it is perfectly logical that we interpret this alignment as a 'special connection' or, as we like to call it, 'love'. Now, this can equally be a friendship or a romantic relationship. From this state of being, of course we cannot feel one with everyone, because we see them as others, those who are outside of our own existential experience and we only 'connect' to those who match our own current state of being.

However, this is just the surface of our awareness. What lies below, and deep down, is knowing, feeling, experiencing existence, not as a duality of self and other, but as a singularity in which there is no self and other, but only oneness. From this state of being, the oneness we experience with everyone and everything else, this state of pure and unconditional peace, joy, and abundance, that is real love. True love, being the expression of oneness, transcends colours, shapes, circumstances, space and even time, because oneness means just that – one with everything that was, that is, and that could ever be.

Hmmmm. So if I don't love that sick pervert who kidnapped and abused a little girl, I don't love my own family, is that what you're saying?

Yes, that is exactly what I am saying. The thing is, this feeling we have towards some people but not towards others is not love, no matter how hard we try to convince ourselves otherwise. We can call it many names like affection, sense of belonging, familiarity, parental instinct, emotional comfort, social programming, support, duty, dependance, need, attachment, social obligation, etc., but not love. Why else do you think people get into fights with people they supposedly love? Why do you think people get angry at those they say they love? Why get disappointed in someone you are supposed to love? Why do we sometimes feel like we need a break from people we 'love'?

I don't know.

Simple, because that is not love. As long as you feel yourself as an absolute individual, disconnected from everyone and everything, only able to 'connect' with few other absolute individuals, you will continue to have these love/hate, hot/cold relationships where you are over the moon one minute, only to be sad, disappointed, angry or even depressed, the next minute. As long as you maintain the belief that love, as well as happiness and bliss, are these on-and-off things, you will not be able to experience them.

But you can't be happy all the time. As a matter of fact, without sadness, there is no happiness, because if we didn't experience sadness, we wouldn't be able to recognize happiness. We need all our emotions.

That is true only in the illusion. In the illusion, we convinced ourselves that good and bad, happiness and sadness, light and dark,...are interconnected and interdependent. The notion is that we understand and appreciate one quality because we experience its opposite.
Books are written about it and religions and movements are founded on these foundations, where contrasting

forces are seen as complementary and necessary to achieve balance. In psychology, it's called dialectical thinking, where two opposing truths can coexist, such as recognizing that happiness is meaningful because we know sadness. Bullshit!

All those are just excuses to keep the illusion existing and us sleeping. As long as you keep believing in that bullshit, you prevent yourself from remembering that your and everyone else's natural state is only and unconditionally, goodness, happiness, bliss and love, and that opposites of those are just an illusion that makes us forget who we all really are.

Sounds great in theory, but I don't understand how it can be that someone who does something so horrible as kidnapping and abusing a little, innocent girl is pure goodness, happiness, bliss and love. How could I ever love someone like that?

Let's put it this way, imagine that, on the day of your birth, you had been mistaken for another baby of the same race and gender, and you ended up living in a totally different family in, quite possibly, significantly different circumstances. In this case, there is not a shred of doubt that you would feel towards those people, exactly the same way you feel about your family today. This means that family and the sense of belonging to a family is not determined by genetics at all. It's just a matter of where you were raised. This further means that every person in this world, potentially, is your father, your mother, your sister, your brother, your son, your daughter. Even that 'sick pervert who kidnapped and abused a little girl', from your question. If that person were, indeed, your brother or your son, he would, very likely, not be a 'sick pervert'. He would probably be a man with some very serious problems. In that case, you would still, no doubt, condemn his actions as atrocious, but you would quite possibly still 'love' him as your brother or your son.

That's true. We somehow always find more understanding for those who we consider closer to us.

Definitely! Which is pure love bullshit!

You see, to love, means to feel that we are more than just a body with an ID. To love, is to open ourselves to the all-encompassing abundance that is our true essence. To love, is to recognise others as more than just fellow human beings. To love, is to feel others as our other parts. To love, is to feel one with others, and I mean all others. To love, is to open our eyes to see that we are this eternal and indestructible force that even life itself is made of and that death, pain, destruction or trauma are just illusions. From this love state of awareness, from this love state of being, the man from your question, who, as you said, kidnapped and abused a little girl, is also a being of love, but lost in the depths of his own illusion of darkness. In many ways, he is no less a victim of his condition than a girl is a victim of his condition's actions. When you enter the love state of being, you will see that clearly. Love can't even perceive pain and trauma, let alone feel them. How could it? Love is eternal abundance and absolute unity. For love, there is only joy, bliss and peace. Everywhere, in everyone, and for everyone.

Wow! Huge!

When you allow yourself to experience that love state of being, you will deeply understand that there is no difference between loving yourself, loving your family, loving the man from your question, loving every other person on the planet and loving everything else. In the love state of being, you just love. Not anyone, or anything in particular. Your state of being is love, and all that you perceive, all that you feel and all that you do, will be love.

That sounds absolutely amazing! Like home.

Exactly!

Tell me, how can I increase that awareness of oneness and also my ability to forgive?

Easily! Every time you find yourself challenged to believe in oneness, just say, think or write: 'We are all one, we are all one, we are all one'. And when you catch yourself judging someone, just say, think or write: 'We are all innocent, we are all innocent, we are all innocent'.

OK. How many times? Three?

No. As many as you like. You can't do too much. There is no such thing as a love overdose.

Hehe... I get it. Only if we talk about love bullshit.

Yes! Even a tiny bit of love bullshit is already an overdose.

Makes sense. Thank you!

You are welcome!

I need to admit, I am struggling with 'we are eternal and indestructible', and 'there is no death, pain, destruction or trauma', that you have mentioned before, and I can't stop thinking about it. I can't absorb it. I can clearly see how our forgiveness and sense of unity make us all feel better, which means less war and more peace in the world. But how can you say that death doesn't exist if it's more than clear that people die every day?

Do they?

What do you mean by 'do they'? Where do you live?

On my own planet, haha. The planet of my perception. No, seriously now, how do you know that other people die?

How do I know that other people die? What kind of question is that? It is obvious when someone dies. They stop moving, their heart stops working, they stop breathing...so many proofs of death.

Those are all just proofs that their bodies die. But how do you know they die?

What do you mean?

Their consciousness. Their self-awareness?

I don't know. No one can know that. Those are invisible. We can't know what's going on with consciousness or self-awareness after the body dies. I suppose it's a question of belief.

Absolutely, and I would say that any belief is a question of choice. Don't you agree?

A hundred per cent. Can't be anything else but a choice.

Exactly! We all choose to believe in something or not. Even when we were raised to believe in something, once we become adults, we decide if we still believe in that or not.

That's true.

So, would you say that believing in your eternity and indestructibility makes you less stressed?

Definitely.

Which makes you more calm.

Yes.

Which makes you more healthy.

Most probably.

Which makes even your body live longer and definitely gives you a happier life experience.

Fair enough.

So can we agree that the choice to believe in our eternity and indestructibility is a more intelligent choice than to believe in our vulnerability and weakness?

Yes, we can!

I already told you, everything you perceive as reality is like a dream. Which includes your body and other people's bodies. Because you sleep, you believe that what you see in your dream is true. That is why you believe in separateness and not unity, in death and not eternity, in vulnerability and not indestructibility. I am not asking you to believe in all that, I am suggesting you to believe in all that, because, as we already concluded, that is the most intelligent choice. So give it a go and see if your life changes once you adopt this new perspective of reality. I am sure you will immediately feel more peaceful, joyful and abundant. You will start to experience real love. You will start to remember who you really are. Try it for a minute. Not more. Can anything bad happen if you give it a go for only a minute?

I suppose it can't.

Great. So let's go. Repeat after me, like we did before: I am whole.

I am whole.

I am eternal.

I am eternal.

I am indestructible.

I am indestructible.

Now again! I am whole.

I am whole.

I am eternal.

I am eternal.

I am indestructible.

I am indestructible.

Now try to say it and believe it. Feel it! I am whole.

I am whole.

I am eternal.

I am eternal.

I am indestructible.

I am indestructible.

You can close your eyes if that helps you focus on how you feel. Keep repeating it.

I am whole. I am eternal. I am indestructible.
I am whole. I am eternal. I am indestructible.
I am whole. I am eternal. I am indestructible.
I am whole. I am eternal. I am indestructible.
I am whole. I am eternal. I am indestructible.
I am whole. I am eternal. I am indestructible.
I am whole. I am eternal. I am indestructible.
I am whole. I am eternal. I am indestructible.
I am whole. I am eternal. I am indestructible.

**I am whole. I am eternal. I am indestructible.
I am whole. I am eternal. I am indestructible.
I am whole. I am eternal. I am indestructible.
I am whole. I am eternal. I am indestructible.
I am whole. I am eternal. I am indestructible.
I am whole. I am eternal. I am indestructible.
I am whole. I am eternal. I am indestructible.
I am whole. I am eternal. I am indestructible.**

Yes, you are!

Wow!

How do you feel?

Absolutely amazing! I can't believe it. It worked again. It really did. It didn't at the beginning, because I was just repeating the words without involving myself emotionally, but after you reminded me to believe it and feel it, something started to change in my body. Every time we do these kinds of exercises, when I repeat these positive sentences, I physically start to feel great and I still do feel great.

Yes! You literally changed your body's chemical process. Our emotions are a series of chemical reactions within our brains, controlled by the complex cooperation of neurotransmitters and hormones. There are four main chemicals in our brains that play a significant role in our positive moods, which are serotonin, dopamine, endorphins and oxytocin. The brain controls the release of certain chemicals, called neurotransmitters, which communicate with other areas of the brain to stimulate or calm us. This then has an influence on our mood, emotions and behaviour.

That's why you said that we are 'Emotion-aholics'!

Yes. We are. We are addicted to patterns of chemical reactions adopted in our first seven years of life and/or before, but now is the time to change that. It's the time to boost the production of more positive chemicals, than the ones we are used to producing.

That's a good idea! It's strange, though. That amazing feeling I achieved through affirmations is now starting to wear off.

That's understandable. Repeating positive affirmations for a minute can't change all your subconscious programs. It is more complex. I am happy you were able to feel it at least for a little bit. Now you know how to do it and that it is not difficult at all. Once you get that, everything else is about persistence. Repeat any of those affirmations I taught you, as often as you want to or feel like you need to. Wait, you look worried. What did you let into your mind now?

Yeah. I was wondering, what if I really convinced myself that we are eternal and in the end, we are not?

And? What will happen? Thanks to your belief in your own eternity, you will live your non-eternal life, happy and healthy. Isn't that the point? If you don't choose to believe that you are eternal, you will live your life in fear of death, you will take everything too seriously and probably make yourself suffer for nothing. Wouldn't you agree that it's better to die completely, after living a happy and healthy life, than stay alive after your body's death and realise you wasted your life on fear and worries about nothing?

That's true. Does that mean that we are not our body and that we don't need to take care of it?

We are definitely not our body, but we should still take care of it. The body is your soul's coat and also your soul's transport device in this reality. In the same way you take care of your coats and cars, you should take care of your body. You want your body to work properly and for a long time, just as you want your car to work. A healthy body helps you experience this special adventure called life, in a better way.

That's true, but to be honest, I somehow love this life, this body and everything nice that a body can experience. All physical pleasures. Come to think of it,

I'm not even sure I care so much about eternal life if it's not a physical one.

Now you sound like a small child wanting to protect their pennies, while their parents are trying to explain that they are an heir to an estate and assets of billions of pounds.

What do you mean?

Do you remember how you felt every time you applied positive affirmations?

Yes. Wonderful.

I know I only explained what happens on a physical level, in your brain and your body, but experience goes beyond physical. There is no physical pleasure that can be compared with a real state of bliss. No one even can explain that state. It is beyond words and beyond anything that our small brain can understand.

Does that mean that our body is limiting us?

No, because you are much more than your body. A body can't prevent you from experiencing anything. Your mind is much stronger than your body. Mind over matter. Didn't you hear about it?

Yes, of course. So, does that mean that we don't need a body?

The need is a little bit too strong a word. Not 'need', as such, but I would say that a body definitely comes in handy.

Whaaat?

Yes. I already told you that all these horrors in the world, or better said 'in this reality', are a reflection of our inner state. It's a 'hell' that we create. Taking into account that the material dimension is a little bit slow, I would say it's helpful.

What do you mean slow?

It takes time to mirror all we think. Don't you think that's handy?

Not sure if I follow you.

Think about all the horrors that only parents think when they are worrying about their children. Now, imagine that all that manifests immediately.

What a hellish world that would be!

That is why I told you that worrying has nothing to do with love. It's a big love bullshit! Having in mind how powerful we are, we are very lucky to be in this slow dimension. It is giving us the time (which is also a part of this dimension's illusion) to remember who we are, and to stop creating these horrors around us.

Are you saying that we are guilty of everything that's going on around us?

Guilty? No! Guilt doesn't exist. Guilt is also a part of the illusion that we should release. But whatever is going on around you is created by your mind.

Horrible!

No, it's not, because it is just an illusion, but being in this slow dimension is giving you the 'time' to learn how to change it, how to create a nicer reality.

But why are we creating this horror?

Because we don't know that we are creating it. Most of us believe that what's going on to us has nothing to do with us, and the truth is, it has everything to do with us. We just need to switch from our victim role to the creator role. We are much more powerful than we think we are.

But I am not thinking about bad things and they are still happening to me.

The fact that you are not aware of thinking about them, doesn't mean you are not thinking about them. They are your subconscious thoughts, you know, the ones created when you were little. But more than thoughts, you should become aware of your feelings. Those that you are suppressing every day, pretending that everything is OK. Those that you miss, every time you blame someone else for them. Those that you hide behind alcohol, drugs, video games, falling in love, etc.

Wait. Wait. How can you put drugs and falling in love in the same basket?

Because it's the same. By falling in love and taking drugs, we are lying to ourselves about how we feel.

How can I lie to myself about how I feel when I fall in love, when it's more than clear that I fell in love? I feel excited about seeing and spending time with that person and I feel butterflies in my stomach even when I think about that person.

Exactly because of that. Falling in love is not falling in love, it is falling into the illusion. The feelings that you concentrated on one person should be spread to every person equally (including you), then and only then can be called love, otherwise, it is a love bullshit.

Are you telling me I shouldn't fall in love anymore?

No. I am not telling you that. You can fall in 'love', the same way you can have a drink and play video games, as long as you are aware of that being just an illusion and not something real. It's like a treat that you can enjoy as long as you are in control. When the illusion becomes reality for you, then you are lost.

I know, but when I am in love, I really feel good and when I have a drink, I really feel more joyful. How can something so real, not be real?

Drugs, drinks, games, falling in love, and even some medicine, give you a false feeling of good. The forced one. One that is not from the inside, it is from the outside. That is like a loan. You don't have money, so you borrow money from the bank, and you feel good because you have money and you can buy what you want, but after you buy it, and after the excitement passes, you become depressed because you are now in debt.

Are you telling me that all loans are bad?

No, I'm not. Nothing is bad or good. I'm not judging a loan or anything else. All that is a part of this game called life, I am just telling you how to win this game, how to play it happily and healthy. The loan is not a problem, you create a problem when you convince yourself that you have what is not yours. That makes you wake up in debt, not being prepared for it. The same with the false feelings that you might get from drugs or drinking. You are waking up tomorrow in debt. You are literally depressed for much more time than you enjoyed the day before. So most of the time, it is not worth even trying it, because the price is too high. On the other hand, I would say, if you are really aware of what you are doing and what you are going to pay for it, and still want to experience it, go for it, but have in mind that every second spent in going deeper into the illusion, is a second less towards awakening. So try whatever you want, but keep in mind that nothing from the outside of you can give you the happiness and satisfaction that you can reach from within, and, once you reach them, they will be real and will last as long as you want. Everything else has its end, which starts with paying off the debts.

That's why many relationships end when falling in love dies.

Exactly! They were based on the illusion, on enjoying the internal chemical process that falling in love gives, and also on the illusion that the person in front of you is special and better than others, which makes you feel special and better than others, which makes you feel very bad when you start to realise that that special person in front of you is not so special. Don't you see? When we rely our self-worth or happiness on anything external, we sign our penalty. Sooner or later, we will stop lying to ourselves about the perfection of the person that we have in front of us, who can also be a friend or a family member, not just a partner. This will make us doubt ourselves, because, subconsciously, we convince ourselves that we are worth more for having this nice friend or partner. No we are not! Our value is unconditional and as long as we think differently, we will look for external signs to prove our value, which is complete self-love bullshit.

So what do we need to do to convince ourselves that we are unconditionally valuable?

The same thing you had to do to convince yourself that you are peaceful, joyful and abundant or that you are whole, eternal and indestructible. Keep repeating it to yourself until you believe it, or better said, until you remember it. I am suggesting morning and night moments of stillness and silence in which you are going to repeat it in your head as a mantra. The more relaxed and calm you are before you start, the easier it will enter your subconsciousness. That's why it is very good if you create a place in your home that you will decorate specifically for that daily activity and only for that. It can be a corner in the room or a piece of furniture on which you can put a candle, a nice picture, a sculpture or anything else that helps you relax and feel good. Once you create that peaceful corner, try to be as disciplined as possible. You are about to train your subconsciousness how to think differently, how to stop believing in all that it lived when you were a small and vulnerable child. The subconsciousness is like a badly trained pet. It is time for retraining, for reprogramming. That is why it is very helpful if you sit in this peaceful corner, every morning and night, at the same or at least a similar time, if it's possible. It will help, but it is not in any way a condition.

So do your best and forget the rest. Once you are there, you can use nice relaxing music, a relaxing scent, or whatever else can help you feel relaxed. Then you can start with any breathing exercise, it can simply be conscious breathing. Staring at the flame or flower also helps. The more relaxed you are, the better, but if you have a bad day and you can't relax, don't worry, you can still sit and repeat positive affirmations.

Which ones would you suggest for the self-value issue?

I am important, I am worthy, I am valuable, I am deserving, I matter.

I am important, I am worthy, I am valuable, I am deserving, I matter. I am important, I am worthy, I am valuable, I am deserving, I matter. I am important, I am worthy, I am valuable, I am deserving, I matter. I am important, I am worthy, I am valuable, I am deserving, I matter. I am important, I am worthy, I am valuable, I am deserving, I matter. I am important, I am worthy, I am valuable, I am deserving, I matter. I am important, I am worthy, I am valuable, I am deserving, I matter.

I feel nice after this! I definitely can see the self-value problem in myself. I would say I can see it in everyone I know. It is such a deep program that makes us complicate our lives for nothing. I can clearly see how

the world can be a much better place if we all deal with it.

Exactly! That's the point. Now, I have to mention, that if you catch yourself starting to feel more important than others, or that you matter more than others, it is time to add to these affirmations 'also' or 'we are all'.

What do you mean?

I am also important, I am also worthy, I am also valuable, I am also deserving, I also matter. Or, we are all important, we are all worthy, we are all valuable, we are all deserving, we all matter.

Why even start with the other one if those are better?

They are not better, they are only closer to the truth, but most people live in such an illusion of lack of value that using 'also' or 'we are all' will not make them feel the affirmation. Do you remember when I said how feeling is more important?

Yes. Now I get it. It's like a medicine. For strong cases, stronger doses, but if your case is not strong, take a smaller dose of medicine. As with any medication, too much can cause an imbalance.

Exactly, and you can apply this to any affirmation that starts with 'I am', any that we already mentioned, any that we will, and any that you will ever come up with. All of them will one day become 'we are all'. When that moment comes, you will be able to relax about the doses, because you can never have too much of truth or too much of pure love. It is like medicine vs a healthy way of living.

I get it. It makes sense. Do you think everyone will have the time for those morning and evening practices that you suggested?

Time is not an issue, only an excuse. Don't forget that we are 'emotion-aholics', we are addicted to our suffering, which doesn't help to let it go. To make this morning or evening practice happen, only 10-15 minutes is needed, sometimes five, if you are in a rush. So if you take ten minutes in the morning, and ten minutes at night, that will be 20 minutes less sleeping or 20 minutes less on your phone, but those 20 minutes will heal your body and mind, so each of us has to decide for ourselves, if we want to be happy and healthy, or keep suffering.

That sounds like an easy choice. I will definitely give it a go. Everything makes sense and doesn't cost any money, so I can't find a reason why not to try it.

Be aware that your subconsciousness will find a reason. Probably a million reasons why you should not start these morning and evening practices. Also, it will probably give you many reasons why you should not start today, but the following day. Then, when the following day comes, it will tell you again how it is not the right time and how it would be better to start some other day.

Is there anything else that can help me reprogram myself even faster?

It is not about speed and goal. Try to relax and enjoy the process. Try to be aware of your feelings. Don't suppress them. You don't need to go around and tell everyone how bad you feel, because that will not help at all, it can only make it worse, but try to be honest with yourself. Accepting your own feelings is the first step towards change. There is no reason to feel bad about it, because, as I already told you, it is not your fault. Whatever you feel, you got it mostly while you were a little child, functioning mostly with your subconscious mind. So everything you lived, everything you saw, everything you felt, or someone next to you felt, during your first seven years of life, got stuck in your subconscious, because the subconscious mind can't choose or reject. It absorbs any information and feelings coming into it. So please, don't blame yourself anytime you don't feel well, and don't try to ignore it, because everything that comes from the inside is trying to tell you something. It's like your small self is sending you messages from the inside out. Don't try to ignore those messages/feelings. They are important. Listen to them. Feel them. Accept them, and then let them go.

How?

Just let them go. For example, when people start to feel sad, many will pretend they are not sad. They would even convince themselves that they are not sad, maybe even try to hide it with a drink or two. I know sadness is an uncomfortable feeling, but, as with the muscle cramp, you need to face it in order to let it go. So immerse yourself in the feeling and even ask yourself why you are sad. I am sure there are deeper emotions behind it. Whatever you find out by talking to yourself, accept it with no sense of guilt and recognise that whatever it is, it was given to you when you were a child or even before, and then consciously decide to let it go. Acknowledge that you don't need it anymore. You can even give thanks for it because it probably taught you something, but now it's time to let it go. So with this acknowledgement, you start to feel a release, you will even be able to imagine it going away, which is a wonderful and liberating experience.

What if I am sad because something sad is going on in my life?

No, you are not. There is no such thing. Whatever is going on in your life that 'makes' you sad, is just a trigger, a reminder that helps you realise what is still in your subconscious program that needs to be released.
Do you remember this: 'We don't feel what we see, we see what we feel'?

Yes, I do, but what if someone close to me died?

No one dies, we already spoke about it.

OK. OK. But still, they left this reality so I will not see them for a while.

So?

They are special to me and I will miss them.

There are no special people, we are all equally special which makes us very unspecial. Only your perception of them being special is making you believe that you are sad because of the loss.

Sorry to interrupt you, but aren't they special because they raised me or built a life or a company with me or raised my kids with me? They were close to me. Isn't that enough to make them special?

Are you telling me that you are special?

No, I am telling you that they are special to me.

'Me'? There is no 'you'. There is only oneness and its equally valuable parts. Because you think you are a special part of oneness, you think your people are special too. You don't need to be special to be valuable and important. You are already valuable and important, just because you are equally a valuable part of the oneness.

But doesn't that make me not important? I mean, all of us.

No. You don't need to be better than others to become important. Oneness is incomplete without any and each of its parts, so we are all important and very valuable to each other because we make oneness complete, we make us complete. We can't exist separately, nor can we exist without any of us. Isn't that enough for one to feel important and valuable? To feel they matter?

Well, yeah.

So, it's time to stop competing and fighting each other, and to start understanding that we are each other. It is also time to recognise our true value through our inevitable importance in the union of all of us. We can stop convincing ourselves that we are special, only to feel important, and start to remind ourselves that we already are important. We are unconditionally important. There is nothing to do or nothing to become, to be important. Importance is our essence.

So, only your perception of yourself and your people being special is making you believe that you are sad when you lose them, regardless of whether they left the country or this reality. The thing is, you were sad before you lost them, the sadness was a suppressed feeling of yours, and you use your loss, or better said, your belief about your loss, to feel sadness again. Can't you also be at peace with their leaving?

Probably. But why did you say 'belief about your loss'? It's not a belief if they move to another country or a reality, it is a loss.

Because loss is an illusion. We are all connected all the time. Even if someone leaves your country or reality, your essence is always connected with their essence. You can't be separated. You are one, you have always been one and you will always be one. We are all one!

So what should I do if I still feel sadness?

Face it. Embrace it. Don't suppress it. Acknowledge that it doesn't have anything to do with what's going on in your reality now, but with what happened when you were a child.

What about other feelings, like anger?

It's the same. Whenever something or someone in your life triggers your uncomfortable feelings, be aware they are just messengers trying to help you. It doesn't matter how annoying the person in front of you seems, they are there so you can wake up from the illusion.

Are you telling me they are annoying me on purpose and with awareness of me needing them to be annoying?

No. They are not annoying at all. You perceive them as annoying only because your false beliefs need more food, your subconscious program needs another shot of annoyance. It's the same with everything else. It doesn't matter how annoyed or angry you might be with someone, your feelings are yours.

So what should I do with them? Should I express my anger in order to not suppress it?

No. Every time you do it, you will lose the message that the trigger is bringing you. Also, it will stink.

What?

Stink. Uncomfortable emotions are like farts.

Farts?

Yes. How much does your fart have to do with a person next to you?

Haha…nothing.

How much does anything around you have to do with a fart itself?

Nothing.

What is the source of any fart?

A gas?

No. That's the fart itself. The source?

A food?

Yes! A food that you ate, but when?

I don't know.

Sometime before the fart occurs?

Yeah.

So, it is something in the past that you consumed, and after some time of internal digestion, gases are created and they have the urge to go out, from inside out, you would say from nowhere. Isn't it?

Yes.

Can't you see the connection? Whatever is coming from inside out, no matter if it's anger, annoyance, farts or anything else, it has nothing to do with people or situations around you. If you let it out, it will stink.

Haha...I get it.

Do you think it's nice to put this innocent person in front of you in this very unpleasant situation?

Hahaha...of course not.

Whatever you 'ate', I mean lived, absorbed, experienced, when you were a child or even before, it has been digested in your mind and body, and now it has the urge to go out. Whatever it is that is coming out, has nothing to do with anyone around you, except for the fact that those might help you to remember that something is inside and wants to go out, but that doesn't make them deserve to smell your stinky fart.

Haha...I get it, but isn't it unhealthy to keep it inside?

One hundred per cent correct! The same as a fart, it's better to let it go. So what do you do in the case of farting?

I go to the toilet or an empty room.

Same thing. Find a quiet corner and let it go. If it's too strong, hit a cushion, scream, jump... If it's tolerable, sit with it, to define the feeling and then let it go.

What about happiness? It also comes from the inside out.

Happiness doesn't stink. You can, and should, share it as much as you can. It is also healthy to let it go. Like a burp, it might annoy some, but it doesn't stink, and it might make someone laugh too.

Haha...that's hilarious! I love it!

Burrrp!

Hahaha....

I told you! Haha... Isn't this life beautiful when we are relaxed and happy, when we share laughter and good moments with others?

Yeah! Definitely!

That's love! Just being, sharing, connecting!

It's easy with someone as relaxed and happy as you are, but as soon as someone annoying and messed up enters the room, I can't help but lose it.

It's because you rest your happiness on others. Your happiness is yours and no one can take it from you.

What if someone is talking to me directly, with very rude manners? That's very personal!

Only if you take it that way.

How can I take it differently if they talk to me?

Just be aware of them expressing their suffering, trying to liberate their pain. No one who is rude is happy. Have you ever heard a happy person saying: 'Oh! I am so happy! I fancy hurting someone!'?

I get it, but why do they speak to me? What do I have to do with their pain?

Nothing at all, but they don't know that. They got an urge from inside out and you were there. They fart!

Hahaha...

Now, you can choose to smell it, I mean, take it personally, or hold your nose until the smell passes.

That would be great if I were able to remember that in the moment when I needed it.

Don't worry! If you don't, that's probably because that person is your trigger, your messenger and is there so you can realise what's going on inside you. If their farting motivates your farting, you know what to do, and if their farting is just their farting, and you are cool with that, then the lesson is not yours, only theirs.

Interesting! Is there anything I can do to become less sensitive to their fart smell?

Of course! Work on your own awakening to remember, as soon as possible, who you really are and who others really are. As long as you are sleeping, you are dreaming an illusion about yourself and that person being completely separate.

So, I suppose you don't recommend any kind of boundaries in relationships?

Boundaries? Bullshit! Another self-love bullshit! Boundaries only reinforce your illusion about us being separate. You can't understand what real self-love is if you don't know who your 'self' is. If you think you are what you see in the mirror, then boundaries are a logical self-love move for you, but when you wake up and realise that you are everyone and everyone is you, then you will realise that there is no difference between love and self-love, between loving yourself and loving others, and you will realise that when you don't love someone, you actually reject one part of yourself, or that you are not loving your complete self.

Wow! What should I do then in a hurtful relationship? Stay in it and keep suffering in the name of love?

Of course not. Love and suffering don't have anything in common. They are completely opposite. First, use any 'hurtful' relationship to heal yourself, your inner child, by listening to the message that this person is bringing you. Once you deal with yourself, you are ready to move on, not because you are escaping from a hurtful relationship, but because you don't want to support the other self, continuing to hurt themselves.

Uh...wait, I am lost.

I believe you. Let me explain myself better. If you think someone is hurting you, that is only because you forgot who you really are, how indestructible, eternal and powerful you are. You preserve that hurtful relationship because you are sleeping, you live the illusion of your vulnerability. The other person in the relationship is also sleeping, and also living their illusion of vulnerability. Now we have both sides thinking that the other side is trying to hurt them on purpose. Both are triggering each other. When one of the two sides decides to search for a real love, and starts to realise that the other person is not hurtful, but lost, that side will forgive and release all their traumas that this particular relationship is teaching them. Once one side reaches that real love, if the other side is ready for awakening, the real love will also make a change in that other side of this relationship. If the other side is not ready for a change, but rather stays in the illusion and refuses to wake up, even though they were motivated by real love, then the first side, the awakened side, is leaving the relationship. But they are leaving because of love and not because of hate or fear, or better said, from the place of love and understanding, not from the place of judging and blaming.

Are you suggesting, then, to create healthy boundaries?

No. There is no such thing as healthy boundaries, because boundaries are something that you build to protect yourself, something that you build because you believe you need to protect yourself, something that you build because you believe you are weak and you need protection or boundaries. I am talking about staying in the relationship and using it to heal your traumas and leave the relationship only if your healing didn't heal the other side, because if it did not, you need to leave in the name of love, to respect that person's timing. You can't force anyone to wake up. Everyone has their timing. You can only work on your awakening, which will eventually result in others waking up too. The more you work on your awakening, the more others will be inspired, or better said, the other parts of you.

I get it. So it is not what we do, but from which place we are doing it. I remember now you were telling me about it. Building boundaries comes from the place of scarcity. Giving space and time to someone is coming from a place of abundance.

Exactly! Absolutely correct!

So the only thing I can do is keep myself in the state of abundance, or as you said it: 'peace, joy and abundance', as much as possible.

Precisely!

Which I can achieve, by reminding myself who I really am, through morning and night practices that include positive affirmations and all-day-long self-observation in order to recognise any hidden emotion, so I can name it and let it go.

Exactly! You can also set alarms or some other kind of reminders to practise affirmations during the day. For example, by only repeating or writing all, or some of them, every hour or half an hour. That's useful especially when you sit with the emotion and realise that, for example, behind the anger triggered by someone accusing you, is actually the hidden sense of guilt. Try to repeat that day or even the next one, as often as possible: 'I am innocent, I am innocent, I am innocent', or 'it is not my fault, it is not my fault, it is not my fault'. Whatever makes you feel better.

OK, but isn't it better to say positive, rather than negative affirmations?

It depends. If your program of guilt is too strong, 'I am innocent' will not make much sense, because you will not believe it. On the other hand, saying to yourself 'It is not my fault' can really bring a feeling of innocence. What we need here is a feeling. Words of affirmations don't count. Only the feelings that they create do. Many people will start with 'it is not my fault', and after a while will naturally switch to 'I am innocent', that's why I always offer both and let people choose.

Try it yourself! Repeat a few times one and then a few times the other and tell me which one convinces you more, which one makes you experience more internal peace.

It is not my fault, it is not my fault, it is not my fault, it is not my fault, it is not my fault, it is not my fault, it is not my fault, it is not my fault, it is not my fault. I am innocent, I am innocent, I am innocent, I am innocent, I am innocent, I am innocent, I am innocent, I am innocent, I am innocent.

Yes. You are right. I find the first one more convincing. My guilt program is definitely big.

I'm not surprised. Guilt is the biggest program of all. Everyone has it and a lot of it. Insecurity is right behind. If you work on just those two, you can't go wrong.
Guilt is such a strong program that will automatically make many people reject whatever I am mentioning here, only because once they are about to see that there is an easier and happier way of living their life, they need to face the fact that almost everything before wasn't, which is the perfect trigger for their guilt program.

That's crazy! It's not their fault that they didn't know better.

Of course not! Triggers never make sense but can be so strong and uncomfortable, even unbearable that people rather stay in the unknown, than face the trauma of guilt and make their life a more joyful and abundant experience.

Are you saying that the guilt program is the reason why people don't embrace changes more often?

Yes.

Spooky.

Totally spooky, but it's much easier to be right than face the guilt.

Give me an example.

Imagine that a long time ago, you had an amazing friend who, at some moment, became your trigger. The friend 'made' you feel all sorts of uncomfortable feelings, which weren't produced by your friend, but by your traumas, but you didn't know that at the time, so you believed that friend made you feel that way. Because you couldn't bear to feel that way anymore, and you didn't have knowledge and awareness of how to use the trigger to heal your traumas, you stopped seeing that friend. You thought that was best for you, even though it never felt one hundred per cent like it was, but you just didn't know better. After, for example, 20 years, I am telling you about triggers and how we don't feel what we see, we see what we feel, which makes you understand, that because of the lack of this knowledge, you didn't just lose the message that your friend was bringing you in form of a trigger, but you also lost your very good friend. That revelation itself is a huge trigger for your guilt trauma, which makes you convince yourself that everything I talked about is nonsense.

Uuuu, I get it. It makes sense. I might even reject your help before I realise that your help itself is triggering me.

Exactly!

We could call this a psychological inception, haha...

I couldn't have said it better myself.

You said that insecurity is also our biggest program. The first big one after the guilt one. I can see that in myself too. It is very strong. I can see it even more than guilt.

That's because the guilt is more sneaky. It hides where you would never search for it.

That's interesting. So, what should I say to work on insecurity?

I think one of the best affirmations for releasing the insecurity program is: 'I am confident and I am enough', but I also recommend: 'I am beautiful, I am great and I am powerful'.

What if I am not beautiful?

Everyone is beautiful. Beauty is in the eye of the beholder. For me, everyone is beautiful!

Do you mean physically?

Even physically, but that is not what I am focused on when I look around. I can't tell you what colour eyes people in my life have, or even if they have glasses or not. Soooo not important to me. I am seeing their inner beauty, their potential, their power, the one that even they themselves can't see.

That's amazing! That must make your life extremely beautiful. I mean seeing all those beautiful and powerful people around you.

Indeed.

Wow! Let me try these new affirmations!

Let's go! Repeat after me. I will repeat each of them three times. After saying them loudly, take a few seconds to feel each of them.

Okey dokey!

I am confident, I am confident, I am confident.

I am confident, I am confident, I am confident.

I am enough, I am enough, I am enough.

I am enough, I am enough, I am enough.

I am beautiful, I am beautiful, I am beautiful.

I am beautiful, I am beautiful, I am beautiful.

I am great, I am great, I am great.

I am great, I am great, I am great.

I am powerful, I am powerful, I am powerful.

**I am powerful, I am powerful, I am powerful.
I already feel better!**

And that is only on a conscious level. I can't even explain how important it is to do all this 'affirmations' thing early in the morning or anytime just after meditation, when your mind is half conscious and half subconscious. I've practised for years, many different things that work on the conscious mind, but I have never experienced so many, and quick changes as I have since I started applying the methods that work on a subconscious mind, and when I did it on a daily basis. It is incomparable.

So discipline is the key?

Definitely! If you have any problems with discipline, that's only because your old subconscious program is fighting to survive. It is convincing you that today is not a good day to start, that this technique wastes your time, or that you are not progressing. Whatever is needed to make you stop. You should ask yourself: 'Do I really want a change? Am I ready for a change? Am I ready for more peace, joy and abundance? Am I ready for more health, opportunities and success?'

Of course I am.

Says your consciousness. Do you know what your subconsciousness is saying?

Probably the opposite.

Correct! That is why it is so important to keep this in mind and do whatever is needed to be more persistent than your old subconscious program. There is an old you created from childhood traumas and a new you that consciously decided to release those traumas in order to become more healthy and more happy. We could say that the new you is trying to kill the old you. The old you will fight hard to survive. Its life is in danger.

Oh! I love this analogy! Makes me feel more motivated to beat the old me.

That's great, but be careful not to hate or be afraid of the old you. The old you needs your love and understanding, the same as a hurtful partner. Leave them both from love and not from hate or fear.

I think I get it all. I will try to apply it to my daily life. I am only afraid that discipline might be my issue. I am not a very disciplined person. I am more like a free spirit. I like to do what I want, when I want.

That's the biggest nonsense I have ever heard and I have heard it before. Every time you declare yourself as a free spirit person is because you are not free at all. Being free is being able to do whatever, whenever and thoroughly enjoy it no matter what it is. That's true freedom. When you have anything that you can't be asked to do, it means your traumas are putting limits on you and you are accepting those limits as real even though they are a huge illusion. So every time you do only what you fancy doing, you are defining yourself as small and limited, and only when you start to face those limits and step out of your comfort zone, your freedom starts to grow. So there is no better tool for freedom than discipline. Discipline means you are doing it also when you don't fancy it, because you understand that what you do is good for you, and you don't want to let anything stop you, not even your traumas, I mean your own subconscious program.

That makes sense. Do you really believe that after repeating those affirmations on a daily basis and to our subconscious mind, we really can change? For example, to become a happier and calmer person?

I don't believe it, I know it! I lived it, as have many people around me. But it is not about change. You are not becoming happier and calmer, you just remind yourself what you already are. You were always happy and calm. That is what you are. Peaceful, joyful and abundant. You just forgot it, and you live an illusion about not being that. That's why I said that it is not a change, it is more like a wake-up.

Is there any affirmation that is better than others? More powerful or more beneficial?

No. You can affirm whatever you want. I always recommend: 'I am peaceful, I am joyful and I am abundant, because I am love' as a basic everyday or every-hour reminder, because it covers all, it reflects our essence, but anything else we mentioned or anything else that you come up with is also great. You can't go wrong, as long as you train your mind to think positively and you train your body to feel it.

What if I can't feel it?

If you can't convince yourself, even for a few seconds, that you are what you are affirming, then try to adjust. For example, if you are saying 'I am peaceful' at the moment when you can't really feel it, because you are, for example worried, try to repeat it several times and if nothing changes then adjust the affirmation to 'I feel peace', which is a little bit easier to believe because it doesn't define you as a peaceful person but expresses a moment in which you feel peace. If this adjustment also doesn't work, after several repetitions, try 'every second I can feel more and more peace' or 'every second I am closer to my peaceful state of being'. Use any kind of adjustment that will help you feel less stressed at that moment. As long as it works, it is good.

It might also happen that whatever you say, whatever you do, you don't achieve any kind of change, which is difficult, because in most cases persistence will bring results, but let's imagine that it is one of those days that not many things can help. In that case, don't worry, do your best and forget the rest, but don't stop yourself from trying. Even when your conscious mind is rejecting it, your subconscious mind will receive it, because the subconscious mind is not capable of rejecting anything, that is why we have so much crap inside from our first seven years of life, and that is why it is very useful to read, say or even better, write affirmations in the first five minutes after waking up, while the subconscious mind is still reachable.

Cool! I wonder if it works for 'I am peaceful, I am joyful and I am abundant', why not use it for 'I am rich'?

You can use it for whatever you want. You can program yourself to whatever you fancy. The reason I am not suggesting to start with 'I am rich, I am wealthy, money loves me and comes to me easily and effortlessly', is not because I don't believe it works, but only because the world is full of rich and unhappy people. Do you want to be one of them?

Of course not.

So that is why I suggest you start with affirmations that will make you feel better, but those will also manifest good things in your life because feelings are the ones that manifest. You can't convince your subconsciousness that you are abundant and deserving and not having in your life as a result, events and things that prove that. Whatever you experience and live in your life right now, is a result of your old programs, of your subconscious self-belief. You can't have a subconsciously bad opinion about money and actually have money in your life. If you don't like money, you don't have money. Resolve all your issues about money and money will come. On the other hand, you can have a very good relationship with money but, for example, not with your sense of innocence, which can make your life a living hell, full of money.

I get it, but I can do both at the same time. Can't I?

Of course! Affirm whatever you want, just don't become another 'prick' in a fancy car. *(smiling)*

Hahaha...OK. I promise I won't.

Good. *(smiling)*

What do you think the source of the money problem can be?

Same as with love. A belief that there is a limited amount.

But money has a limited amount.

Does it?

Of course. We can count exactly how much money there is in the world. Love, we can't count.

We just believe we can count it, but we never tried, so we can't be sure. Even if we could count it and get to a certain amount, that amount would be only a reflection of our past beliefs on how much money we deserve. This doesn't mean that if we change our beliefs about money we can't create more.

Are you telling me that all money problems in this world are not because a few greedy people took most of it, but because most people believe they don't deserve it?

Yes.

So there is not a limited amount of money, there is only a limited amount of created money, which is also not limited because we can always create more.

Exactly!

But I always believed that, if I get more money, I will make someone have less. This belief has always stopped me from thinking more about money. I even feel guilty every time I charge for my services.

I know. Money, as a limited thing, is one of the biggest illusions of this world. It is not just you who believes that way, which is obvious, as most of the people on this planet are poor and not rich, but can we agree that it is not only about money? It is more about what you can buy with it, as I am sure no one would like to have lots of money on Mars where you can't buy anything.

Completely agree.

So what would you call that state of having money but also having options to buy? Or even better, having everything you want for free?

Abundance.

Exactly! Abundance is what you are looking for, and not the money itself. Soooo many rich people live scarcity and many poor people live abundance.

How can rich people live scarcity?

Easy. They can have lots of money, but they can feel empty inside. They can also not appreciate what they have, and not feel gratitude, joy and abundance. On the other hand, they can be identified with their possessions which can make them live in constant fear of losing what they have, and so on and so on.

Interesting, but how can poor people live abundance? They are literally poor. They might even miss the basic things in life.

It doesn't matter how little you have, you can always choose to be grateful for the little you do have. Gratitude automatically makes you feel abundant. If you trust that life is always giving you exactly what you need and when you need it, you are abundant. If you don't measure your own value by what you possess or what you achieved, you are abundant.

Are you sure that gratitude makes you feel abundant?

I am, but don't believe me. Try it!

How?

Repeat several times: 'I am grateful', and see how that makes you feel, but try to believe what you say, try to really feel grateful.

OK. Let me try! I am grateful. I am grateful. I am grateful. I am grateful. I am grateful. I am grateful. I am grateful. I am grateful. I am grateful. I am grateful. I am grateful. I am grateful. I am grateful. Wow! That really makes me feel abundant.

You know what the funniest part is?

What?

Their entire lives, people pursue all kinds of things and achievements, only because they want to feel abundant. What they don't see is that the feeling itself is right in front of their noses, or, better said, right inside their heart. They just need to choose to feel it. With a little bit of gratitude, they got it.

Now try this! I am grateful for my life.

I am grateful for my life.

I am grateful for my breath.

I am grateful for my breath.

I am grateful for this day.

I am grateful for this day.

I am grateful for the earth.

I am grateful for the earth.

I am grateful for the sun.

I am grateful for the sun.

I am grateful for love.

I am grateful for love.

How are you feeling?

Wow, really abundant! No matter how little we have, we can always find things to be grateful for. 'The richest person is not the one who has the most, but the one who needs the least.'

Good one! Abundance is a state of mind. It has nothing to do with what you have or you don't have. It is our essence. We just need to remember who we really are. There is nothing we need to do, there is nothing we need to be, to experience abundance, because we are already everything and everyone. We are abundance itself.

Does that mean I shouldn't have money and nice things?

No, it doesn't. You can have as many nice things and as much money as you want, but work on your inner state. Once you achieve a constant state of abundance, money will not be important. Money or any other possession. You will realise that you can have it or not, but that will not change your state of being. You will always be abundant. It's the same as with love. Whether you love someone or not, is not defined by what you do or say, it is defined by your inner state. If you vibrate high and allow unconditional peace, joy and abundance to flow freely through you, everything you do from that state is love.

So I am allowed to be ambitious?

You are allowed to be anything you want. The question is, what do you want?

I want to be happy.

So don't be ambitious.

I am confused. Didn't you just tell me that money and possessions can't change my state of being?

I did. They can't, but we are not talking about possessions here. We are talking about being ambitious. I am telling you not to be ambitious, because you can't be ambitious and happy, and you want to be happy, don't you?

Yes.

Ambition comes from scarcity and a belief that in order to become valuable, you need to achieve something. As I already told you, probably several times, and I will probably tell you a few more times because it's very important: In order to be happy, to experience real joy, you don't need to do anything or become anything or anyone, you just need to become aware that you are already everything and everyone.

That scares me a little bit.

What do you mean it scares you?

If I really let myself believe that I am already everything and everyone, such peace will get into me that I will sit and do nothing. I will waste my life.

I can see what you mean. That's the old, false you talking nonsense. Don't take it seriously, because when you reach that state of internal peace and abundance that I am telling you, you will be so fulfilled, so abundant, that you will naturally want to share. That sharing, seen from the outside, might seem like an ambition, but it is actually an expansion. It feels like an urge, like an internal call to give, a natural instinct to share and give because you are so abundant and so happy that you think you are going to explode if you don't share it. You become more confident, more creative, and more kind, that natural reaction is to create, to serve, to build, to expand.

What if I reach this state of happiness but I don't have anything to give?

You always have something to give. You can give your time, your kindness, your happiness, joy and smiles. You can give a good example, you can give your attention, high vibes, love, etc. The more you give, the more you will have, but only because by giving you are confirming that you are an unlimited source of everything. When you give in to giving, you will find that love is not about being loved, but about loving.

I have been giving my whole life and never got anything in return. People just take me for granted and whatever I do is never appreciated or recognised. Where is the love in that? How can you not feel disappointment and bitterness for everything that you have done for others and given selflessly without even so much as a 'Thank you.' How can that be love?

Only unconditional giving is love. Whenever we give, expecting something in return, expecting to gain something or feeling like we took something away from ourselves to give to others, we only further build and strengthen the illusion of separateness and scarcity which is the very reason we feel the drama and victimism in the first place. It is only when we give from a place of abundance, that we reconnect to the limitless source of love inside us. It is only then that we realise that it's not about us loving others and others loving us and doing things to prove our love. It's about the unity with everyone and everything, experiencing that connection and the eternal, indestructible abundance that arises from it.

What about rich people who created money from ambition and not from expansion? Are they going to be unhappy forever?

Of course not. Having money doesn't prevent you from working on yourself. They just need to stop identifying their value with their bank accounts, feel the traumas they are hiding behind their money, and face them, the same as I already explained to you. They can use their affirmations to reprogram their old self and use their triggers to recognise their inner old patterns. We are all equally capable of working on ourselves, it doesn't matter how much money we have or not.

Mentioning now triggers, you remind me of something that is on my mind. I wonder, does letting go of all our traumas mean that we can reach a state where nothing touches us?

That's right.

Doesn't that mean to become like a rag?

No. Your association of not having traumas with a dull person only proves how identified you are with your traumas, how much you believe that you are your dramas and that when you get rid of them you will become insensitive and boring. Your old self only convinced you of that, because it's it, not you. Your old self is drama, you are peace, it worries, you rejoice, it lives scarcity and you are abundance. The absence of drama is not the absence of all emotions, but only those that are uncomfortable, those that are not healthy for you. I know it's hard to imagine that state from this perspective but believe me, it's really beautiful and completely indescribable. Only when you get rid of the self that you are not, can you truly experience what you really are, and believe me, it's worth the effort. I know that your old self, I mean, the false self, convinces you of the opposite and tries to dissuade you in many ways, but don't believe me or it, try it. Just try a little. Just try to resolve one trauma and you will see for yourself that what remains behind the trauma is anything but dullness and insensitivity. So remember how you felt when you just pretended to be who you really are, which is joyful, peaceful and abundant.

Yes. At times I managed to feel so wonderful that I don't even remember if I've ever felt that way before.

Yeah! That one and many more beautiful emotions come when you let go of what you are not. I mean, you remember them. Apart from the idea that you will become empty and emotionless, has it occurred to you that you will also become stupid, naive or perhaps vulnerable if you let your uncomfortable emotions go?

Yeah! How did you know?

I went through that too. I know what it's like. I didn't always have this awareness. I worked to get here, the same thing I'm teaching you to do.

And what about people who have some disorders that make them much more sensitive than most people, or they don't have any filters, so it's much harder for them not to react to their triggers?

It makes no difference. They can make the same progress as you if they don't hide behind their condition.

What do you mean?

Many people with such and similar disorders are adults, and aware of their challenges. They can make a lot of progress, and the fact that they don't have a filter, and are more sensitive, can help them see their traumas even earlier, and more easily than those whose brains work in such a way, that enables them to hide and suppress their traumas very well. Also, most of them will find it difficult to accept their own responsibility for their emotions, because the diagnosis is a very good excuse for not taking responsibility. It's the same with hormonal disorders in which emotions run wild. That's the little self, screaming out of you to be heard. It's time to stop ignoring it and help it heal.

And what about those whose condition is much worse and might not be aware of themselves at all?

Of course, they are not able to apply this kind of work to themselves, but those around them are. If the people around them resolve their traumas, especially their parents, their progress is inevitable.

Interesting. Thank you! Can I ask you something else, please?

Whatever you want.

You mentioned before that love is absolute and that we can't love someone and not love someone else.

Yes.

If it's really either love everyone or not love anyone, how do we choose our life partner?

A life partner doesn't exist. Why should we, in the sea of people, walk our entire life just with one of them? If it happens that we find one that walks our entire lives in the same direction as we are, then great, but if on our life path, different people come and go, that's also great.

OK. So it doesn't have to be one, like a lifelong partner, but even in the short term, how do we

choose one and not the other one, if we love everyone equally?

We don't.

We don't what?

We don't choose. We shouldn't choose. It's not fair, and it's also not healthy.

So we shouldn't have any relationships?

No. I didn't say that. I only said that we shouldn't choose who we are going to have relationships with.

So how do we end up in a relationship?

By accident.

By accident?

Yes! I believe that relationships should happen spontaneously between people who recognise they are heading in the same direction at the same speed.

I don't understand.

Imagine that you are walking from Brighton to London.

OK. I did.

Now during your walk, you notice that someone else has been walking in the same direction for hours already. After some time, you start to talk, as it's natural, you are not going to walk all the way in silence. That would be awkward.

True.

So you walk, you talk, you share, you help each other, you support each other...and then you realise: 'We are in a relationship!' You didn't choose each other, you just happened to be on the same path. You weren't looking for each other, because you don't need each other. You weren't in need or bored, you were both individually fulfilled and happy. You were just walking your individual paths, living your lives, enjoying your lives, but somehow your similar way of walking and obviously the same direction made you connect.

I get it. So if that person went from Brighton to Eastbourne we wouldn't even meet?

Correct!

So I don't need to search for a relationship?

You don't. You just live your life as a whole person, and a relationship will happen to you.

As a whole person?

Yes, because nothing is missing from you. You are whole and complete. You are not a half that looks for its other half.

But sometimes I feel like something is missing from me.

That's because you forgot that you are whole and complete. You are already connected with everyone and everything, but only because you identify yourself with your body, you believe that you are separate and lonely.

Yes! Sometimes I am lonely.

Then all you need to do is remind yourself of your wholeness and remind yourself that you are enough. There is nothing and no one you need. You, yourself are already all that there is.

But how can I remind myself of my wholeness?

You can use positive affirmations again: 'I am whole, I am complete, I am connected with everyone, we are all one', but you can also do a daily meditation in which you visualise your connection with everyone. That will make your loneliness disappear.

Let's do it now!

OK. Let's do it!

Relax your body and pay attention to your breathing. Be aware of the air coming inside and outside of your body.

Now imagine a spot of light in the middle of your chest. Imagine the light spot is so bright that it makes your whole body full of light.

Now the light from your chest becomes so strong that it can be seen even outside of your body.

As you keep breathing and relaxing, the light becomes even stronger and fills the entire room.

Now your light can be seen outside of the building.

Keep growing your light, spreading it all over the country, lighting every single person on its way.

Your light is so big and widespread now, that it covers the entire continent, and finally the entire planet.

Don't forget to imagine all those people that your light has just touched. They can feel your light, but you can also feel theirs.

This mutual invisible connection is unstoppable. It is not there only when you think about it, it is there non-stop. Bring to your body the feeling of deep connection with everything and everyone. It is a satisfactory feeling of wholeness and completeness.

Absorb it!

Embrace it!

Stay with the feeling as, at the same time, you become aware of this room and your physical body.

Take a few deep breaths, without losing the feeling from the meditation, and open your eyes when you are ready.

Wow! That was so relaxing and highly satisfying!

I am glad you felt it!

I can still feel it.

Keep it as long as you can and when you lose it, you can always repeat the process. Some days will be easier than others but it's still worth doing.

I get it. So relationships should happen by accident, we should just live our happy lives and let relationships happen spontaneously by only recognising someone is heading in the same direction and with the same speed as we are.

Exactly, but that is only on the conscious level, on a subconscious level, there are no coincidences and everything is happening for a reason.

So they are not happening by accident?

They are not, but you should take it that way, to let go of the control. Every time you try to control, you block. So live your life, love everyone, and let life bring you what is best for you.

But what if more people walk from Brighton to London?

Many people walk from Brighton to London, but they have started sooner or later, or they walk faster or slower than you, so you will meet many of them, but you will not have the opportunity to talk with them all, or at least not for a long time, as your journeys do not synchronise.

What if more people are walking in the same direction but also at the same speed as I am?

They are, as well, but your vibrational field attracts the one with the same vibration.

What?

In our travelling analogy that means: you will not be able to notice others as much, maybe because of some trees and bushes in the way.

What about marriage? I understand that any kind of relationship happens spontaneously, but how do we get married spontaneously?

When you honestly think about it, you will agree that love does not need marriage. It's not like, oh you guys love each other, you need to marry; or they are not married, oh well that's because they probably don't love each other. Bullshit. Don't you agree?

Of course!

Now, the truth is that people marry for a plethora of reasons other than love, like pregnancy, a sense of doing the right thing, financial security, social pressure, fulfilling an expectation, legal reasons to obtain certain rights, fear of growing old alone, etc. Of course, people also marry to celebrate their relationship and to share with their partner their intention to walk the journey of life together. The point is, we could go on and on naming all kinds of reasons why people marry and none of those reasons would be love.

Hmm.

The truth is, if there were nothing to gain from marriage, socially, legally, financially and any other 'lly', it's highly likely that most of the marriages would never happen. I would go even further and say that, without those loveless marriages, there would be a lot more happy people.

Probably. Are you trying to tell me that marriage is not a good idea?

No, I am not. There is nothing wrong with marrying if you are not doing it to gain something from it and if you are not doing it 'to have and to hold from this day forward, for better, for worse, for richer, for poorer, in sickness and in health, to love and to cherish, until we are parted by death.'

What's wrong with that? Isn't that the point of marrying to promise each other those beautiful things?

No, it's not. It's what society makes us believe it is, but actually it is nothing but a big fat lie at the very beginning of the marriage. No one can promise something like that and no one should.

So what do you think we should vow during the wedding ceremony?

An intention to walk the paths together, as long as that makes sense and not a day longer or shorter. An intention to be honest and kind. An intention to work individually on ourselves in order to grow together and also support each other on that path. But you should agree with me that every couple should be able to do all that without marrying. It should be a thing from the first day of the relationship and not from the wedding day.

That's true, but why did you say 'an intention to be honest'? Shouldn't be that a promise?

You can't promise what you are not sure that you are going to be able to do. That's already some kind of lie.

What do you mean by 'can't promise'? You lie or you don't lie.

It is not that simple. Most people search for the truth all their lives. How can we be truthful if we don't know yet what the truth is? Because of all those traumas inside us, we see our reality differently. Traumas act as filters and make us believe in things that are not. Also, the famous 'guilt' makes us lie to ourselves too. Sometimes we are so convinced that lies are true, that we are not aware of lying.

I get it. We lie more than we are aware of.

Exactly! To ourselves and to others. That's why we can't promise that we are not going to lie much less vow it, but we can vow our intention to it. Because all things that I suggest to vow during the wedding ceremony should be part of the relationship from its first day, I think marriage is not a necessary thing, but only an extra experience in life, something nice that doesn't change relationships at all. The problem starts when someone takes a marriage as a false security of love, which makes them suffer if it comes to an end.

You mean if one of the partners changes their mind and, at the halfway point, decides to go to Dover or to stay in Crawley, instead of heading towards London?

For example, yes.

So what happens in that case?

Nothing. They thank each other for the nice journey and everyone follows their new path.

Sounds so simple when you say it that way.

Because it is simple. We just make it complicated.

Why do you think we are doing it?

There are plenty of reasons. Most of the time we identify with a relationship. We rely our value on it, so when it comes to its end, we think one part of us is dying with it, which is the purest form of bullshit. We also rely our wholeness on it and our happiness in general, because we believe we are not enough or we don't know how to be alone. If we could just remember that we are already valuable, whole and enough, unconditionally and in our essence, there would not be any drama or pain around relationships ending.
Because of the social pressure and all these false beliefs around relationships, we don't recognise when a relationship naturally comes to an end. We force it by trying to change the other person, by trying to convince the other person to go to London, even if they had already decided to go to Dover, for example.

What if going to Dover is obviously the wrong choice, so we are trying to help that person not make a mistake? Can't convincing in that case be actually loving and caring?

Who are we to know what a right or wrong choice is for someone? There is no such thing as a right or wrong choice anyway. Stopping others from following their path has nothing to do with love, no matter how much we convince ourselves that we love that person and that we are just trying to help them. That's just another love bullshit. Love is accepting and allowing. Love is absolute respect, even if it seems obvious to us that a person is doing something 'wrong'.

Are you telling me that I should let someone, whom I love, hurt themselves?

Exactly! That's only true love and it applies to any kind of relationship. We can offer ourselves as help and support, but allow others to choose if they want help or not, and not take it personally if they don't. Anyway, what does hurt mean? Sometimes pain is something that people need to feel in order to wake up from the nightmare. The only reason why we should want to keep someone next to us is a selfish reason that is coming from our own trauma. Love would never do that.

What if they are parents? If people were more flexible in terms of their relationships, that means that most of the relationships would be short-term. Wouldn't they?

I don't think so. I would say, that when people embrace flexibility of relationship length, that actually helps them stay together in longer and happier relationships. Also, when you truly understand that there is no better partner, you stop doing the nonsense of leaving someone for someone better, because there is no better. But, if it happens that the paths of someone's parents separate, and they decide to follow their natural flow, that would make them lovingly separated parents. They would still love each other, which would not be the case if they stayed together only because of the children.

So it's like a reverse psychology? I let you go which makes you not go.

You might see it that way, but I believe that people are scared of the promise of 'forever', which is understandable because it's not natural. Once you release the pressure of 'forever', people invest more in the relationship. Did you realise how many couples stop being kind to each other and only take care of themselves once they get married?

Yes! Many people do that.

Most of them do that because they feel safe in their 'forever' marriages. On the other hand, if they enter the marriage with a promise that they will check if they are on the same path every single day, that would motivate them to work on themselves constantly and in every aspect.

Makes sense. Can you please explain something to me from the previous answer?

Of course! Whatever is needed.

First, you said 'There is no better partner' which makes me understand that whomever we are with right now, no matter how uncomfortable or painful the relationship is, that's the best one for us. Then you said 'They decide to follow their natural flow, that would make them lovingly separated parents', which means separation can be our natural flow. Those two things seem very opposite. Which one is correct?

Both. I am glad you asked this question. That means you are listening carefully. Both of these sentences are correct and I will do my best to explain how that is possible, with them being so opposite. Basically, it depends on the situation. The shortest answer would be as always, to check what place your idea for breaking up is coming from.

How?

Ask yourself: 'Do I want to break this relationship up from love or from hate, from abundance or from scarcity, from peace or from unrest?' And then listen to yourself, feel yourself, and be honest with yourself. If you hear a voice in your head telling you: 'You are going to be better without this person'. Don't listen to it. It's a trap. If you feel that the reason for your unhappiness is the person in front of you, you are wrong. Whatever it is, that this person does that makes you feel uncomfortable, it is not because of that, it is always because of something that is already inside of you. Some trauma, a wound that you need to heal. Use this person as a messenger, as a mirror, to heal yourself and then after it, see if you still want to leave that person.

How would I know that the 'after' has come?

Probably, whatever that person was doing that was making you feel uncomfortable, will stop; or they will still do it, but you are not going to have an emotional reaction anymore to it. I am not saying you should agree or approve whatever that person does, but you will at least be at peace with it, because it will not be connected anymore with your wound. Your wound will be healed.

I know we already talked about it, but can you please remind me what exactly I should do to heal it?

Don't react, don't suppress, sit with it and when you find out what the emotion is or/and what false self-thought might have caused it, attack it with its contrast.

For example?

If your partner is criticising you, you might recognise that your feeling about it is anger, caused by feeling not appreciated and not respected, which makes you doubt your self-value. Attacking it with a contrast would be to work on your self-value and self-worthiness. Bring yourself into relaxation mode with meditation, breathwork or staring at the dot, and repeat or write 'I am worthy, I am valuable' as many times as you want. Do it also when you wake up and before you go to sleep, as that would be the closest moment to your subconsciousness if you don't have time to meditate.

What do you mean by 'staring at the dot'?

Ah! The black dot on the white paper or wall. I call it 'the door to a new dimension'. I can't even explain with my words how beneficial it is. It is an amazing exercise for improving focus and calmness, but it is also much more. Draw a dot on a white paper and tape the paper to the wall or wardrobe, then sit in front of it and look at the dot for at least five minutes per day. Try to slowly and gradually get to 20-30 minutes per day. The little black dot will change your life. Don't take my word for it. Try it!

Sounds interesting. I definitely will! So all this emotional healing is the reason why we should stay in the relationship even when it's not comfortable.

Yes.

But how do we know that someone else wouldn't be even better for that?

There is no better or worse. The one you have in your life is the one who came to your life for a reason. Your vibrational field attracted that person. Your wounds, your traumas, needed that person. Your inner child chose that person in order to heal itself. I know it can sound unbelievable but that is the way everything works.

So what is the moment in which we separate in love?

To separate in love, both partners should heal all traumas that were triggered by that particular relationship. In that moment, they might recognise that their paths are separating and, with love, they release each other.

Does that mean that all relationships have to come to their end, once both parts heal traumas connected with those relationships?

Of course not. They are free to stay together and enjoy themselves after they heal, but it might happen that their paths naturally separate.

What if just one of them heals those traumas triggered by that relationship?

The healed side should offer help to the other side, which might not even be necessary because the other side should already be inspired by the pure love from the healed side. If it's not, then the healed side is offering help, but if the other side rejects it, the healed side has to leave, otherwise its staying would support the other person's pain, which pure love would never do.

How do you know that you and your partner are on different paths?

To be able to recognise paths, one should first heal, because traumas can trick them about paths, and convince them that paths are different, only to avoid the pain from the healing process. Once both partners heal, if they can't find any similar interests and most of their daily plans don't match, because their passions and goals are completely different, it means they are on different paths. They will naturally split in love.

So what if that lovingly split couple has children?

Children should be taught that every adult in their lives is a potential guide, not just their biological parents. How many times does it happen, that one person who is not ready to have children, ends up having them and leaving them, and then, into those children's lives, enters someone more than ready to lovingly lead them through their early paths? Not everyone who has children is awake enough to realise that raising them is their responsibility. On the other hand, children should be taught to love and respect their biological parents as they are, and respect their timing in the awakening process. Which is why they chose their parents at the end of the day.

'Chose their parents'? What are you talking about?

I truly believe that we choose our parents before we are born. I can't prove that being true, of course, but it just makes sense and helps understand parents' role in our awakening. It also helps us to be thankful for every loving moment as well as for those challenging ones they gave us. It actually helps to release all the bullshit of fighting with our parents and trying to change them.
We didn't come to this world to change our parents. It is not our responsibility. No one can change anyone anyway, because there is nothing to be changed. They are already perfect, they just don't know that yet, because they live in the illusion of who they are. But you can't do anything about it, except work on your own awakening. When you learn the useful tools for your own awakening, you can always share them with your parents or anyone else if you check before that they want it too.

So I can't share the useful tools with them if they don't want to, even if I know they are good for them.

Why would you? You will do that and because they didn't want it, or they weren't ready for it, they will put them on the side and not use them. The same as with a partner. We should respect their timing. That's love!

Makes sense. Would you say it is better to travel alone or accompanied?

Neither. Both are equally good ways to travel, I mean, to live your life. Accompanied can be more fun, but also more challenging as no one can trigger you better than your close ones. But don't worry, if you don't have anyone close in your life, you will be triggered by complete strangers. You can't run away from it. What has to be healed, has to be healed. It doesn't matter how much you fight against it, it will find you and it doesn't matter how many people you leave and relationships you break up, it will find you as whatever it has to be healed, it's inside of you, so running is absolutely useless. You can't escape from yourself.

So life is always putting in our way what we need the most.

Yes! Precisely!

What about sex? If we end up living alone, how are we going to have a healthy sexual life?

What do you mean by a 'healthy sexual life'?

Like having regular sex with one partner.

Who says that is a healthy sexual life?

Everyone.

Everyone, like society?

Yes.

Since when is society the one to follow?

Since always.

Who told you that?

What do you mean who told me? Everyone knows that.

You mean everyone, like society?

Yes.

In order to bring any positive change in our lives, we need to start questioning everything we know or do. Just because something has existed for centuries doesn't mean it is still the way to go. We have changed, we have evolved. We can't keep living as if we haven't.

Are you trying to tell me that having sex with everyone is better than what society is suggesting, to have it with one partner and regularly?

No, I am trying to tell you that sex is something that we don't even need anyone for.

What? So now masturbation is the same as sex?

On a physical level, it is. Your body doesn't know the difference between self-touch and another person's touch. Unfortunately, sex is, for many people, a way to confirm their self-value. They believe, that if they achieve to physically attract someone, or give that person pleasure, that makes them better or more cool. Sex is definitely not a good tool to improve self-value and it can be highly addictive, so be careful with it.

What do you mean by addictive?

Sex is like a drug, drink, falling in love...you can easily lose control over it, by hiding your emotional pain behind it. If we become aware of it, we will realise that sex is something that we don't need at all.

What do you mean by 'we don't need at all'? What about physical desire? We can't ignore it!

Well, we actually can, but we shouldn't. We can release it, though, with masturbation or we can transmute it to something else.

Trans...what?

Transmute.

How?

Sexual desire is an energy accumulated in the lower part of your body. Lift it to the heart area and it will become love. Lift it to the head area and it will become wisdom.

Wow! Sounds like magic!

It is! And we are all magicians. Now you can see that sex is not something that we need.

Are you saying that we should forget about sex? Wouldn't that be the end of the human race?

Lack of need does not mean abstinence. Like, when I say you don't need any relationships because you, yourself are more than enough, I don't mean you should just forget about others. I just want to say that the awareness of the fact that you don't need relationships, just makes the experience of being in a relationship all the more enjoyable because it takes away the additional weight of our emotional investment that comes from us viewing the relationship as something important and necessary. The same thing goes for sex.

Does that mean that when we let go of the importance of sex, we will then start enjoying it?

That's right.

But I'm already enjoying it.

Now imagine just how much you will enjoy it then.

Hmmm, interesting. What about cheating?

What kind of cheating?

In a relationship. When someone has sex with another person? Someone who is not their partner.

I don't see that as cheating. Sex itself can't be cheating, as you are the owner of your body and no one should ever think it's theirs. So as the owner of your body, you are allowed to do whatever you want with it. What I would call cheating, is hiding from your partner that you had sex with someone else.

So having sex with someone who is not your partner is not cheating.

No, it's not.

So I can go around and sleep with whoever I want?

Yes, you can, if those 'whoever you want' want it, but why would you?

Hmmm, why would I?

Yes, if you already have a partner and you are happy together, why would you even think about having sex with someone else?

Maybe because I am not happy.

Having sex with others will not resolve that. So why are you not reminding yourself of your unconditional happiness? Remember, your natural state is unconditional happiness, everything else is an illusion. Try to recognise traumas that prevent you from being happy, rather than running away from them into a sexual adventure that may bring you complications in life.

What if I am not triggered by my partner but we have been together for so long that our relationship became boring?

There is no such thing. Either your traumas are tricking you and convincing you that you are bored, just to give you an excuse to create more drama in your life, you know the stress addiction that I was talking about?

Yes! 'Emotion-aholics'!

Exactly! Or you forgot to check if you and your partner are still on the same path. Maybe you even did check, but for some reason, you don't want to face the fact that it is time to move on. Sometimes, people are more scared of being alone, than they are of staying in a relationship that doesn't make sense anymore.

How would you describe a relationship that doesn't make sense anymore?

Like a relationship that doesn't trigger but also doesn't motivate anymore.

Hmmm sounds logical. So fear of being alone can be an issue?

Yes! When people have a fear of loneliness, they force themselves to be in a relationship with a person who is trying to go in a different direction. Because of fear of losing that person, they stay together even though they know it doesn't make sense. It's like you are walking with someone from Brighton to London and in one moment you realise that they have changed their mind and want to turn towards Eastbourne. Instead of letting them go, you hold that person tight, next to you, only because you are afraid to walk alone. So you pull that person with yourself towards London and they pull you towards Eastbourne. What would happen?

We would probably stay in the same place.

Exactly. You are blocking each other from any kind of travelling.

What if my direction is better?

There are no good or bad directions in life. Everything is a game anyway, so there's no point in pushing anyone out of their way. Breaking up a relationship doesn't mean you are going to die and never see each other again. Stay friends, visit each other, call each other, and text each other, but you don't need to walk the same path anymore.

Makes sense. So if I understood this 'cheating' subject well, cheating is allowed but useless.

Exactly! I wouldn't even call it cheating, because it should be like a normal thing.

Have sex with others while you have a partner?

No. Not having it forbidden.

Probably the fact that it is forbidden makes it more desirable.

You got my point! Also, it makes you lie about it, and feel guilty. If you could openly talk with your partner about your challenges and desires, your partner would probably help you recognise all the hidden traumas behind, and maybe even teach you how to heal them and transmute your excessive sexual energy into something different. If you hide it, that only distances you from your partner.

Most people would leave their partners if they knew they slept with someone else.

That's because they made this stupid promise not to do it, so everything around it seems like a betrayal. If this stupid concept didn't exist in the world at all, no one could take it personally. We even have derogatory names for people who get cheated on. That makes it even more embarrassing and attacks even more your self-value trauma.

That's true. Sometimes, it hurts more what others are going to say about us, than being cheated on itself. The power that we give to other people's opinions is immense. I know couples who are together only because they care about what others think.

Yes. Fear of being criticised is bigger than following your own path, it doesn't matter if following your own path means breaking up a relationship or changing a career. How many young people study what parents expect them to study?

Loads.

The question is, why do parents expect their children to study what they think is good for them and not what the children would like?

In many cases, parents don't even know what their children want, because the kids are scared to talk about it, which is probably because their parents didn't give them a chance to do it, because they were very worried about their future.

Was it a worry or something else?

I don't know. I would say they want the best for their children.

They do, but they don't know that they can't know what the best for others is, even when those others are their children. Most parents hide their own insecurity behind their ambition for their children. Children, on the other hand, are not expressing themselves because of their own insecurity. That makes them work in a profession that wasn't their choice, sometimes they even marry someone who wasn't their choice and never change any of those because insecurity made them afraid of being criticised. So many people live lives designed on the expectation of their parents or society itself, only because their self-value trauma is very strong.

What would you suggest to them?

To repeat a thousand times per day: 'I am valuable, I am worthy, I am enough', and add whatever suits their situation, for example: 'It is OK to follow my path. It is OK to be myself. It is OK to follow my passion. It is safe to change my career. It is safe to be alone. I am safe. I am protected. I am accepted. I am loved. I am enough. I don't need other people's acceptance. I don't need other people's approval'. And so on. There is no good or bad affirmation, as long as it helps you release your traumas, fears and emotional pain.

I am very sympathetic to those who have difficult parents. My parents are also that way. They are very tiring. They always think they know what's best for me, that I don't even bother to see them. Actually, I avoid them as much as I can. Our relationship became even more unbearable when I started to express myself. I am done with being quiet and obedient, I am physically getting sick of that.

What made you start to express yourself?

I just realised that I needed to tell them what I think. They can't control me all my life. I had to put them in their place.

Can you give me an example of you expressing yourself?

For example, the other day, they dropped by and found me relaxing on my couch. They immediately started to preach and wonder how I could do nothing. Just because they never let themselves relax in their life, doesn't mean I have to live that kind of life as well.

I agree. And how did you react?

I told them what they deserved. To stop tailoring my life. To stop judging me and expecting of me.

Did you say that calmly or you were upset?

Oh, no. I wasn't calm at all. I was very upset. I was out of my mind. They never stop and I am an adult, they can't treat me as a child anymore.

I completely agree, and I don't justify their behaviour, I am just trying to explain that, in many cases, parents are the source of our traumas, but they are also our messengers. That can be very confusing. First let's understand that whatever they did, and whatever they do, they do it with good intentions. That doesn't mean what they do is from the place of love, but it is the best they know, so there is no point in blaming them for anything. Whatever they did when you were little, however, they treated you, it partially developed your subconscious program, but whatever they do now doesn't have anything to do with how you feel.

I don't get it. So them treating me as an incapable kid doesn't have anything to do with my feelings?

Exactly! Do you remember? You don't feel what you see, you see what you feel.

I know, but it is obvious that their behaviour is annoying.

It doesn't matter how obvious it is, your feeling has never to do anything with what's going on right now in your life, but with what happened in your life when you were a child. The confusing part of this particular example is that the same people were part of the creation of your emotions and are a part of their healing.

How can their stupid behaviour heal me anyway?

It can help you remember what is stuck inside. That's why I said they are messengers. Triggers are messengers and emotions are messages, you just need to listen to them, feel them, and allow them to be.

That's what I did. I allowed them to be, and that is why I became furious and told my parents what they deserved.

But they don't deserve to be told anything else but: 'Thank you'.

'Thank you'???

Yes, thank you for helping me remind myself of what I need to heal. Obviously, you are not going to say that out loud if they don't know what you are talking about, but you are definitely not expressing your anger, because that will make you lose the message. That would be, as I already mentioned, the same as farting.

It can't be the same as farting if it's coming from a place of love.

What do you mean love? You see, talking about something that reminds you of your own emotional pain, draws you in such an illusion, that everything we have just said about love, seems to have disappeared for you. When I say 'fart', I always mean the expression of uncomfortable feelings, and uncomfortable feelings are never love, it is always drama.

I was expressing love towards myself. Finally expressing what I think, for which I never had the courage. I was releasing my traumas by expressing myself. Isn't that self-love? Protecting myself.

Which self, if you and they are one? You are them and they are you. You can't express self-love by hurting your other self. Self-love is the same as love itself because there is no separate self. Also, what kind of self-love is ignoring one's emotions? Taking responsibility for one's own emotions is the greatest form of self-love, and that means not farting to others, but going to the toilet and dealing with it. Every time you fart, you lose the lesson, which means less self-love. Also, the idea that we have to defend ourselves from others, only confirms our weakness, not our strength, and increases our victim role.

I thought that anger exists for a reason, and that, if it's expressed with love, is healthy. It can prevent us from getting ill for not expressing it.

I also agree that anger exists for a reason and that it should not be suppressed, but neither should it be nurtured, it should be allowed to be, but in solitude, not in front of others. Squeeze that fart until the others leave, then fart after. Hit the pillow, scream, jump, shake, dance, and let the anger out, but not in front of others.

So you don't think my avoiding seeing them is good for me? I think I am not ready to be next to them, as long as they make me feel unrest.

They are a part of your healing. I know you've convinced yourself that you're not ready, but you are, you just think you're not. Running away from the pain they make you feel leads nowhere. Allow yourself that restlessness and emotional pain. Face them, but not your parents, your emotions. Every time you face your parents, you run away from pain, and pain is a part of healing. Let that restlessness overwhelm you to bring you messages. You don't even have to call or see them, just think about them. Imagine them and let your emotions overwhelm you.

And then what?

Once you find out what the emotion is, remind yourself that the source of it is in the past. Whatever you can recognize that you are feeling, is just a reminder of accumulated traumas in your body. Now is the time to let it go. Acknowledge it, give it thanks for everything it taught you, and let it go. You don't need that trauma anymore. Then is the time to embrace your new self through affirmations opposite than the trauma you are releasing. Once you resolve the emotions that are coming out when you think about your parents, you are ready to see them. I mean you were always ready, but if you do this previous step it will be easier to face whatever is coming when you are with them.

And what should I do with the emotion they produce when I am with them?

They remind you of?

Yes, they remind me of.

Keep it inside until they leave or until you find yourself alone. Then allow yourself to feel it. Ask yourself how you would name the feeling that is coming out when they treat you like a child.

I don't know.

Give yourself suggestions. Did they make you feel useless, unimportant, incapable...?

Yes, all of that!

You see, you only need to try to guess and when you get to the right answer you will not have any doubt about it. It will completely resonate with the emotion that you feel, but to be able to connect the answer with the feeling, you need to allow yourself first to feel it. When you express your feelings towards others, you lose that opportunity of getting the answers that you need for your healing. Once you get your answers, you can apply your positive affirmation regarding them. Do you have an idea what those could be?

I am useful, important, capable...hmmm...purposeful. Yes! My life has a purpose. I matter!

Brilliant! You got it!

So how should I talk with them when I see them if they still talk to me like I am a child?

Try to understand that whatever they do to you, they are not aware of it.

Shouldn't I make them aware of it?

No, not if they don't ask you to, which is not the case. When you deeply understand that whatever is coming out of their mouths is trauma and not love, you will be able to talk with them with love and understanding because you will not feel attacked, judged or criticised.

I still find it difficult to accept that I should just let them be so unaware. Like I am giving up on them. All that stress they are creating for themselves by worrying about me is killing them.

It is not killing them as they are eternal and indestructible, as you are. Also, you are not giving up on them. Taking responsibility for your emotions will give them the opportunity to follow you. Love is accepting them as they are and giving them space to grow at their own pace, but more than anything, love from your side is giving a good example. It's the same with children as well. With anyone actually.

That makes sense, we can't preach what we are not doing.

Exactly, and there is nothing better you can do to help them wake up from their nightmares than you waking up from yours.

I can accept that easily with my kids, but shouldn't our parents have to be our example?

Who says that parents are the ones who have to be an example? Why wouldn't children be those who set an example for their parents? Remember what I said about traumas? They are also inherited from generation to generation until someone decides to stop them. By taking care of your traumas, facing them and healing them, you are breaking the family chain of traumas. You are the first to awake. Once you do it, that will create a new chain of love towards both sides, your descendants and your ancestors.

That sounds cool, but I still have to find a way to forgive my parents for not doing it for me.

That's very easy if you understand that they would if they knew how. They just didn't know how and they still don't know. Everything they gave you was their best.

Sometimes I just think it's easier to let it go than to forgive.

It may look easier but it is definitely not the way to your happiness. You can't be happy if you are not honestly kind and you can't be kind if you don't forgive. And I am not talking just about parents. We should forgive everyone.

Everyone, everyone?

Everyone!

You seem so nice. I have never met someone so calm and wise as you. What are you, perfect?

Aren't we all?

Maybe in some way we are, but you are special.

I am not. I am an equal part of the oneness. Equal as you are. The only difference between you and me, is that I remembered who I am, and you haven't yet. That's why I am here, to remind you.

Are we all going to remember soon?

In the blink of an eye. Awakening is already in process.

Why is it important to wake up, if everything we dream is an illusion?

Because no one likes nightmares.

Can anyone be lost forever, that never remembers?

Impossible! No matter how much someone tries to sleep, sooner or later they wlll also wake up.

Even those who already left their body, this dimension?

Even those. We are all one, we are all connected and we are all going to be connected.

That's cool! It makes me feel not lonely anymore, and powerful as well. I can strongly feel how this union is

powerful, and how powerful each of us is as its equal part, once we understand this connection.

Exactly! I would say that our only problem is that we are not aware of just how powerful we are.

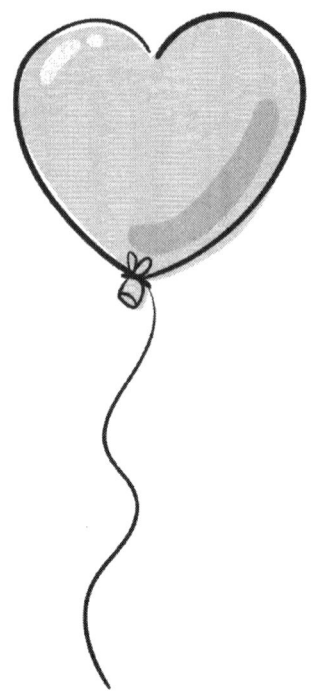

Printed in Great Britain
by Amazon